READINGS ON

LORD OF THE FLIES

Other titles in the Greenhaven Press Literary Companion Series:

AMERICAN AUTHORS

Maya Angelou
Emily Dickinson
Nathaniel Hawthorne
Ernest Hemingway
Herman Melville
Arthur Miller
John Steinbeck
Mark Twain

BRITISH AUTHORS

Jane Austen

WORLD AUTHORS

Sophocles

BRITISH LITERATURE

The Canterbury Tales
Shakespeare: The Comedies
Shakespeare: The Sonnets
Shakespeare: The Tragedies
A Tale of Two Cities

THE GREENHAVEN PRESS
Literary Companion
TO BRITISH LITERATURE

READINGS ON

LORD OF THE FLIES

David Bender, *Publisher*
Bruno Leone, *Executive Editor*
Scott Barbour, *Managing Editor*
Bonnie Szumski, *Series Editor*
Clarice Swisher, *Book Editor*

Greenhaven Press, San Diego, CA

Library of Congress Cataloging-in-Publication Data

Readings on Lord of the flies / Clarice Swisher, book editor.
    p.   cm. — (Greenhaven Press literary companion
to British literature)
  Includes bibliographical references and index.
  ISBN 1-56510-628-8 (pbk. : alk. paper). —
ISBN 1-56510-629-6 (lib. : alk. paper)
  1. Golding, William, 1911–   Lord of the flies. 2. Survival after airplane accidents, shipwrecks, etc., in literature. 3. Boys in literature. I. Swisher, Clarice, 1933–   .
II. Series.
PR6013.O35L643   1997
823'.914–dc21   97-5020
                                                      CIP

Cover photo: Archive Photos

Copyright ©1997 by Greenhaven Press, Inc.
PO Box 289009
San Diego, CA 92198-9009
Printed in the U.S.A.

"I believe that man suffers from an appalling ignorance of his own nature."

**William Golding,
"The Writer in His Age"**

Contents

Chapter 1: The Form of *Lord of the Flies*

Chapter 2: Themes in *Lord of the Flies*

dark element in human nature. Because the schoolboys
fail to confront it and try to control it with the wrong
methods, it is reborn in renewed violence.

Chapter 3: Techniques and Conventions in *Lord of the Flies*

ers and characters find action that surprises them and
behavior that disappoints them.

Chapter 4: Evaluation of *Lord of the Flies*

FOREWORD

*"'Tis the good reader that
makes the good book."*

Ralph Waldo Emerson

The story's bare facts are simple: The captain, an old and scarred seafarer, walks with a peg leg made of whale ivory. He relentlessly drives his crew to hunt the world's oceans for the great white whale that crippled him. After a long search, the ship encounters the whale and a fierce battle ensues. Finally the captain drives his harpoon into the whale, but the harpoon line catches the captain about the neck and drags him to his death.

A simple story, a straightforward plot—yet, since the 1851 publication of Herman Melville's *Moby-Dick*, readers and critics have found many meanings in the struggle between Captain Ahab and the whale. To some, the novel is a cautionary tale that depicts how Ahab's obsession with revenge leads to his insanity and death. Others believe that the whale represents the unknowable secrets of the universe and that Ahab is a tragic hero who dares to challenge fate by attempting to discover this knowledge. Perhaps Melville intended Ahab as a criticism of Americans' tendency to become involved in well-intentioned but irrational causes. Or did Melville model Ahab after himself, letting his fictional character express his anger at what he perceived as a cruel and distant god?

Although literary critics disagree over the meaning of *Moby-Dick*, readers do not need to choose one particular interpretation in order to gain an understanding of Melville's novel. Instead, by examining various analyses, they can gain numerous insights into the issues that lie under the surface of the basic plot. Studying the writings of literary critics can also aid readers in making their own assessments of *Moby-Dick* and other literary works and in developing analytical thinking skills.

The Greenhaven Literary Companion Series was created with these goals in mind. Designed for young adults, this unique anthology series provides an engaging and comprehensive introduction to literary analysis and criticism. The essays included in the Literary Companion Series are chosen for their accessibility to a young adult audience and are expertly edited in consideration of both the reading and comprehension levels of this audience. In addition, each essay is introduced by a concise summation that presents the contributing writer's main themes and insights. Every anthology in the Literary Companion Series contains a varied selection of critical essays that cover a wide time span and express diverse views. Wherever possible, primary sources are represented through excerpts from authors' notebooks, letters, and journals and through contemporary criticism.

Each title in the Literary Companion Series pays careful consideration to the historical context of the particular author or literary work. In-depth biographies and detailed chronologies reveal important aspects of authors' lives and emphasize the historical events and social milieu that influenced their writings. To facilitate further research, every anthology includes primary and secondary source bibliographies of articles and/or books selected for their suitability for young adults. These engaging features make the Greenhaven Literary Companion series ideal for introducing students to literary analysis in the classroom or as a library resource for young adults researching the world's great authors and literature.

Exceptional in its focus on young adults, the Greenhaven Literary Companion Series strives to present literary criticism in a compelling and accessible format. Every title in the series is intended to spark readers' interest in leading American and world authors, to help them broaden their understanding of literature, and to encourage them to formulate their own analyses of the literary works that they read. It is the editors' hope that young adult readers will find these anthologies to be true companions in their study of literature.

INTRODUCTION

Readings on Lord of the Flies provides teachers and students with a wide variety of analysis and opinion about William Golding's first published novel. When Golding won the Nobel Prize in literature in 1983, *Lord of the Flies* had been translated into more than twenty languages and reprinted numerous times. In this novel, Golding introduced the major themes he returned to again and again in the novels that followed, including the limited capacity of science to solve humanity's deepest problems and the mystery and source of evil. Moreover, he introduced a mythlike method of storytelling in *Lord of the Flies,* a form that became a hallmark of his novels. Author John Fowles has said that as a contemporary novelist, Golding has remained "his own writer, his own school of one."

Not surprisingly, criticism of *Lord of the Flies* reflects differing opinions as critics explain a novel that fits no familiar category. Critics chosen for this companion represent a variety of viewpoints on the novel's form, theme, technique, and merit. Though most scholars agree that the novel expresses a dark message about human nature, opinion is divided about Golding's inference that the source of evil lies within humanity and about the story's lack of hope. Critics also disagree on the merit of *Lord of the Flies* while conceding its enduring popularity and its value as a teaching novel. Several scholars call for more research, particularly concerning Golding's art—for example, into Golding's use of color, the effect of animal imagery, and the way Golding handles time. This companion challenges students to try, along with the critics, to solve questions about form and theme. It challenges the curious and courageous to respond to Golding's puzzles with their own analyses.

Several of the scholars in this collection have made extensive studies of many of Golding's works. At least three critics are themselves novelists, and one is Golding himself, who wrote his own critical essay on *Lord of the Flies*. Educators are represented both from England and from America, and one writes from a university in France.

Readings on Lord of the Flies includes many special features that make research and literary criticism accessible and understandable. An annotated table of contents lets readers quickly preview the content of individual essays. A chronology features a list of significant events in Golding's life placed in a broader historical context. The bibliography includes books from the war years that shaped Golding's view of humanity as well as additional critical sources suitable for further research.

Each essay has aids for clear understanding. The introductions explain the main points, which are then identified by subheads within the essays. Footnotes identify uncommon references and define unfamiliar words. Inserts, many taken from *Lord of the Flies*, illustrate points made in the essays. Taken together, these aids make Greenhaven Press's *Literary Companion Series* an indispensable research tool.

WILLIAM GOLDING: A BIOGRAPHY

The publishing history of British writer William Golding extends over a period of fifty-five years, from 1934 to 1989. In his lifetime, he published one volume of poems, twelve novels, three plays, three volumes of nonfiction, and numerous articles and reviews. Besides receiving honorary degrees and Britain's highest literary award, the Booker McConnell Prize, he received the Nobel Prize in literature in 1983. Golding gave lectures and interviews in which he discussed his works and his outlook on life, but he kept his personal life private and he resisted celebrity. In *William Golding: The Man and his Books*, editor John Carey offers this explanation:

> Despite his fame, Golding himself remains virtually unknown—as shadowy, almost, as Defoe. That seems a deliberate choice. He has resisted the temptation (if there ever was one) to become a cultural personality or a TV guru—as, with his commanding presence, and that beard, he surely might have.

Though Golding's mind and soul may still seem like an enigma to many critics, those who met or interviewed him encountered a staunch, congenial but reserved man. Of medium height, Golding had blue eyes, a rough beard, and a stocky build, evoking the image of a Viking. When talking about himself, he seemed shy and humble, slow to acknowledge his accomplishments. Recalling a meeting with Golding just before he received the Nobel Prize in 1983, novelist John Fowles found Golding to be outwardly gentle but occasionally blunt when he disagreed, "a mixture of authority and reserve, with a distinct dry humour, a tiny hint of buried demon; a man still with a touch of the ancient schoolmaster." Golding recognized in himself his own masculine traits, which he described as his tendency to make automatic assumptions and to be aggressive in a chess game; he had, he said, a great need to win. He was a talented amateur musician who played the piano, violin, viola, cello, and oboe. He had once wanted to be a concert pianist, but decided he lacked sufficient talent to overcome the disadvantage of being left-handed.

Golding lived his entire life in southwest England, an area rich in the history of Celtic tribes, Roman conquerors, and Saxon invaders. He was born on September 19, 1911, in St. Columb Minor, Cornwall, a small seacoast village near the westernmost point in England, where remains of ancient tribes can be found among the rocks. He grew up and lived his adult life in Wiltshire, a county known for its downs (the high rolling green hills where sheep graze) and farming villages nestled along rivers. Golding loved the wildflowers and even the dampness and drizzle of Wiltshire, whose rich history has left a plenitude of ruins, from Stonehenge to medieval churches and abbeys to moated castles. In an essay entitled "Wiltshire," published in 1966 in *Venture* magazine, Golding writes:

> I could show you a school that was founded only a hundred years ago yet has on its grounds a mound said to be the grave of Merlin. . . . But then I should tell you what no tourist would have time to discover: there is another road, that runs at right angles to others, though it is invisible. It comes up from the river and goes straight under the foundations of the old house. It is the track along which the stone was hauled from Wales—perhaps about 1400 B.C., when nameless people were *re*building Stonehenge.

England's capital was once nearby Winchester, and the surrounding area contains four of England's most famous medieval cathedrals—Exeter, Winchester, Bath, and Salisbury. Golding knew Winchester and Salisbury cathedrals well and loved them both, but Salisbury was his favorite and became the setting for his novel *The Spire.* Of churches, Golding writes in "An Affection for Cathedrals," published in the December 1965 issue of *Holiday* magazine: "The truth is, we have a primitive belief that virtue, force, power—what the anthropologist might call *mana*—lie in the original stones. . . . Our old churches are full of this power."

GOLDING'S FAMILY

The second son of Mildred and Alec Golding, William was influenced by each of his parents in different ways. From his mother, Golding learned pessimism. She was a strong woman who campaigned for the political and economic rights of women with her husband on the town hall steps, but she also had a superstitious sense that the world is a risky place. The sinking of the *Titanic* in April 1912, when William was seven months old, had a lasting dark and worrisome effect on her, a foreboding which she passed on to her son. Originally from Cornwall, she knew the local Cornish ghost stories and amused her young son by telling them with frightening effectiveness. William grew to be much like her, both in appearance and in personality, similarities that perhaps account for their frequent conflicts. William enjoyed using his wit on his parents, especially his mother—"I gave her a hell of a time"—and described her as a woman with strong emotions and interests, who was "fond of me, but not able to stand me." Golding had an older brother, José, and an adopted sister, a cousin whose parents had died of tuberculosis.

In his 1918 diary, father Alec Golding wrote of his son: "Billy is the artistic member of the family. He is a little rascal." Alec Golding, the most distinguished schoolmaster in a long line of schoolmasters, influenced his son intellectually. Born into a working-class Quaker family, Alec apprenticed as a teacher and studied at night until he had earned degrees to teach science, architecture, and music. From 1902 until his retirement in 1940, he was the science master at the Marlborough Grammar School in the village of Marlborough. In an essay published in *William Golding: The Man and His Books*, essayist Peter Moss fondly remembers the elder Golding's science classes; his lessons were filled with biblical quotes and personal anecdotes to illustrate scientific points. He reproduced textbooks by hand for all of his students and devised experiments using common materials like a sewing machine and household spoons. Golding says of his father, "I have never met anybody who could do so much, was interested in so much, and knew so much. . . . He inhabited a world of sanity and logic and fascination."

BOYHOOD AND YOUTH

Golding's boyhood days had elements of gloom and isolation, aspects he wrote about with humor as an adult. His childhood home in Marlborough, situated next to a graveyard, was a fourteenth-century house with dark cellars and thick walls. Similar to the settings of his mother's Cornish stories, it was a dwelling that aroused his fears of death and the unknown. From the age of seven, Golding compared his home to ancient Egypt, another dark and mysterious place in his imagination. So that he could write a play about ancient Egypt, he set about learning hieroglyphics. The Goldings' backyard garden, which bordered the graveyard, had a chestnut tree on which his father had built a ladder; in this tree young Golding read stories and spied on the world. In "The Ladder and the Tree," published in 1966, Golding says:

> This chestnut tree was my escape. Here, neither the darkness of the churchyard nor this vast pattern of work and career and importance could get at me. . . . Here, stirring the leaves aside, I could look down at the strangers in that world from which we were cut off and reflect on their nature. Safe from skeletons, from Latin and the proper requirements of growing up, I could ponder over or snigger at the snatches of conversation from passers-by underneath.

Golding remembers himself as the kid who never fit the mold of a proper English schoolboy. One of the things that set him apart was that until he was ten, his parents gave him his haircuts. In a 1966 essay, "Crosses," published in *The Hot Gates and Other Occasional Pieces*, he remembers that

> they had not the professional touch; and an unfounded rumor circulated among my school friends, that my parents inverted a basin over my head and cut off anything that stuck out. Thus the word 'basin' was flung at me with that terrible jeering laugh which only small boys can employ effectively.

His early school years, he recalls, were a combination of daydreaming and fighting. His love of reading adventure stories, medieval romances, and ancient myths led to a love of words in general, which he collected "like stamps or bird eggs," he recalls in the essay "Billy the Kid," published in 1966 in *The Hot Gates and Other Occasional Pieces*. During lessons, "I was likely to be chanting inside my head a list of delightful words which I had picked up God knows where—deebriss and Skirmishar, creskant and sweeside." When he was not chanting words, he drew airplanes and ships and, at twelve, tried to write a novel. Recess brought fights; after all, he knew the deeds of Lancelot and Achilles. He recalls in "Billy the Kid":

> Fighting proved to be just as delightful as I had thought. I was chunky and zestful and enjoyed hurting people. I exulted in victory, in the complete subjugation of my adversary, and thought that they should enjoy it too—or at least be glad to

suffer for my sake. For this reason, I was puzzled when the supply of opponents diminished. Soon, I had to corner victims before I could get a fight at all.

Finally, the boys ganged up against him, cheered on by the girls. Hurt and surprised, he recognized his isolation and ran home crying; he burst through the door lamenting, "They don't like me!" In "Thinking as a Hobby," an essay published in the August 1961 *Holiday*, Golding describes frequent sessions in the headmaster's study, where he had been sent

because of the latest thing I had done or left undone. . . .

"Don't you ever think at all?"

No, I didn't think, wasn't thinking, couldn't think—I was simply waiting in anguish for the interview to stop. . . . Clearly there was something missing in me. Nature had endowed the rest of the human race with a sixth sense and left me out.

Eventually, in consultation with his parents, Golding made the decision to conform to rules and study his Latin and mathematics. He graduated from Marlborough Grammar School in 1930 ready to attend Oxford University.

COLLEGE AND WORK

Golding entered Brasenose College, Oxford, in the fall of 1930 intending to study science in accordance with his parents' wishes. After courses in chemistry, biology, and old Anglo-Saxon literature, he knew he preferred English. Though he had a powerful respect for science instilled in him by his father, he finally settled on a major in English literature. While studying at Oxford, he continued to write poems and sketches. A friend submitted a collection of Golding's poems to Macmillan publishers, who paid Golding five pounds and published them in a thirty-eight-page volume called *Poems*. The book was part of a contemporary poets series, which also included the work of the young W.H. Auden. Golding later called the poems "poor, thin things," and when asked in an interview by critic Bernard Dick to comment on the book of poems, he said he did not own a copy. He went on, "But I suppose there's one somewhere. Yes, at the British Museum. The Bodleian [the library at Oxford University], of course. Actually, I'd rather forget it." (In 1981, a copy of the out-of-print little book of poems was offered in the United States at four thousand dollars.)

Golding left Oxford in 1935 with a bachelor of arts degree in English literature and a diploma in education. After the university, Golding spent four years casting about. He began a career in social work and spent his spare time acting, writing, and producing for the Little Theater in Hampstead in London and the Citizens' Theater in Bath. He was more of a hanger-on than a key player, even in these small theaters. Golding taught briefly at the Rudolf Steiner School, a free-thinking place that did not appeal to him. He also taught in Maidstone Grammar School and in the evening taught classes at the Maidstone jail. In an interview with critic John Carey, published in 1986 in *William Golding: The Man and His Books,* he comments on the experience:

> During that time I was in Maidstone I did occasionally—once a week—teach English—but it was more or less the three R's, because most of the prisoners were illiterate. I suppose I must have had some vague idea of doing good. But, thank God, it didn't last.

In 1939, the headmaster of the school in Salisbury asked him to come there. Following the family teaching tradition, he took a job teaching English and philosophy at Bishop Wordsworth's School. Unlike his father, Golding taught not because he wanted to but to earn enough money to keep himself alive while he moved on to other things. In the same year, he married Ann Brookfield, an analytical chemist.

THE WAR YEARS

Golding joined the British Royal Navy in 1940, shortly after World War II broke out in Europe. He first saw action while aboard a minesweeper and a cruiser, and then commanded a rocket-launching ship that helped to sink the German *Bismarck.* His ship was also part of the fleet that participated in the D day landings on Normandy in 1944, but as the invasion force approached the French coast, Golding's ship was separated from the rest of the fleet. In the essay "The English Channel," published in *The Hot Gates and Other Occasional Pieces,* Golding describes the experience:

> I left my first lieutenant on watch and turned in, to be fresh for D-day. He lost the whole invasion—simply mislaid it and then confessed when I came up on the bridge at two o'clock in the morning that he hadn't liked to go any faster because it was so dark.... I found that we were miles west of our position. So we turned southeast and steamed at full speed all

night over jet black waves that were showered with sparks of phosphorescence and possibly loaded with mines. I stood there all night catching up and felt history in my hands as hard and heavy as a brick.

Golding's war experience was a turning point in his life and formed a vital part of his developing outlook. By the time the war was over, he had rejected his father's confident, scientific humanism; he had witnessed war's brutality and had adopted a pessimistic view toward his fellow humans. In "Crabbed Youth and Age," published in 1982 in *A Moving Target*, he explains:

> The horror of the brewed up tank, the burning plane, the crushed and sinking submarine—all that is difficult to describe.... The experience of Hamburg, Belsen, Hiroshima and Dachau cannot be imagined. We have gone to war and beggared description all over again. Those experiences are like black holes in space. Nothing can get out to let us know what is was like inside. It was like what it was like and on the other hand it was like nothing whatsoever.

Even though Golding was actively involved in combat during the war, he found long periods of time for himself while his ships were patrolling. He used the time to read and reread Greek history and literature, which he had learned to love as a child. As an adult, he liked the plays of Euripides and valued the structure of the Greek forms and the Greek view of the psyche. When he returned to teaching after the war, he taught himself the language of the Greek tragedians. To John Carey he explains that "The Greek language seems to me to lie closest to the object. The words, the Greek words, seem to me to lie nearer or perhaps even more *in* the thing they stand for, than those of any other language." Golding was also attracted by the tragedians' inclination to concern themselves with plans and plots with an eye toward the way things will pan out, a technique he used particularly in his first novels.

After the war, Golding returned to Bishop Wordsworth's School, where he brought his military habits and discipline with him by taking charge of the school's Combined Cadet Force. He had the boys wear naval uniforms and led them in a study of knots and seamanship. He acquired boats and taught some of the boys to sail. In addition, Golding continued his enthusiasm for music and drama, participating in the school's music program as a piano and oboe player, a soloist in the choir, and an author and composer of school plays. He never did, however, acquire the enthusiasm for classroom teaching that his father had.

EARLY NOVELS

After the war, William and Ann Golding had two children, David and Judith, and Golding began to write again. He published reviews and essays and wrote three novels that he thought would please publishers, but none sold. He persevered because, as he says, he was "haunted by this desperate, cruel, bloody business of believing I can write." His fourth book was *Lord of the Flies*, which was rejected by twenty-one publishers before Faber and Faber published it in 1954. *Lord of the Flies* drew mixed reviews and sold moderately well in England and America until 1959, when it was issued in a paperback edition. It became immediately popular in college bookstores. Teachers soon discovered that the novel effectively illustrated many elements of literary analysis—symbolism, contrasting characters, recurring events, parallel situations—and it fostered lively discussion about violence and evil. In addition, the book had wide appeal among students. In 1963 Peter Brook produced a film version of the novel.

Because *Lord of the Flies* is rich in complexity, allegory, and meaning, critics have interpreted the work in a variety of ways. In a lecture delivered in Hamburg, Germany, on April 11, 1980, and published in 1982 as an essay entitled "Belief and Creativity" in *A Moving Target*, Golding comments on the flood of criticism:

> I am not going to explicate the book for you. That has been done so often by others, has been subjected to Marxist, Freudian, neo-Freudian, Jungian, Catholic, Protestant, humanist, non-conformist analysis and opinion, has been buried with its author not just in a German reference book [the book erroneously announced Golding's death in 1957] but under a pile of not always sweet-scented international criticism there is nothing left to say. The book yields readily to explication, to instruction, to the trephining [surgical removal of a plug] of the pupil's skull by the teacher and the insertion into the pupil's brain by the teacher of what the pupil ought to think about it. I would like the pupil or anyone else to enjoy the book if he can.

During the second half of the 1950s, Golding published a play and three additional novels, which expand the theme of loss of innocence introduced in *Lord of the Flies*. In 1955 he published *The Inheritors*, the story of Lok, an innocent Neanderthal who sees the destruction of his species by *Homo sapiens*. Golding portrays the armed conquerors as arrogant, murderous, and corrupt, not at all superior to the simple, clumsy Lok and his Neanderthal people. When interviewer Bernard Dick asked Golding if he had a favorite novel, Golding unhesitatingly named *The Inheritors*, "and it is also my best." After the publication of this novel, Golding was invited to become a member of the Royal Society of Literature. In 1956, Golding published his novel *Pincher Martin*, which was republished in the United States in 1957 as *The Two Lives of Christopher Martin.* A spare drama of a shipwrecked man, the book opens with a dead sailor clinging to a rock. The book is written as if his life is flashing before him before he dies. Though he has led a selfish life that deserves few favors, he clings hopelessly to life, crying out for mercy.

In 1958 Golding's play *The Brass Butterfly* was performed at Oxford and then for a brief run in London. Styled as mythic Greek comedy based on his 1956 short story "Envoy Extraordinary," the play humorously expresses Golding's distaste for science. A brilliant Greek inventor offers Roman emperor Caesar a variety of twentieth-century gadgets; the emperor rejects a brass butterfly propeller as useless and a steamship as dangerous, but chooses a pressure cooker as a safe, interesting invention. The conflict lies between the inventor's logical mind and the frivolous Roman court.

Golding published *Free Fall* in 1959. In this novel, the first set in contemporary society, Golding wanted to show the patternlessness of modern life. Sammy Mountjoy, a successful painter, searches for a pattern, or meaning, in his art to impose on his life since he, like his contemporaries, has a rudderless life. In an interview with critic James Baker, Golding says that without a moral system, a modern human is "like a creature in space, tumbling, eternally tumbling, no up, no down, just in 'free fall' in the scientific sense." One of the characters in *Free Fall* is a science master named Nick, who, like Golding's father, is a rational, kindly, atheistic scholar.

FULL-TIME WRITER AND GUEST LECTURER

The decade of the 1960s brought new works and added achievements. From 1960 through 1962, Golding reviewed books for the *Spectator*, a British weekly periodical. In 1960–61, he completed a master of arts degree at Oxford; by then, he was earning enough money from the sales of *Lord of the Flies* to leave teaching and devote all of his time to writing. He wrote two radio plays for the British Broadcasting Company: *Miss Pulkinhorn,* aired on April 20, 1960; and *Break My Heart,* aired on March 19, 1961.

Golding spent 1961–62 as a writer in residence at Hollins College in Virginia, and made a lecture tour of other American colleges.

After Golding returned to England from America, he published two books considered the closing works of the first phase of his writing career. *The Spire* (1964) is about Salisbury cathedral, the cathedral with the highest spire of all English cathedrals (added one hundred years after the cathedral was built). In Golding's novel, set in medieval times, the dean of the cathedral, Jocelin, is told in a vision from God to build the great spire as a prayer in stone. He is warned that the foundation cannot support it, but he forces the project forward. After losing friendships, health, the lives of men, and his own humility, he dies, not knowing if he built the spire for God's sake or his own, if it is sacred or obscene. In 1966 Golding published a collection of essays, entitled *The Hot Gates and Other Occasional Pieces,* discussing people, places, books, education, childhood experiences, and travels.

Golding's writing habits were somewhat unusual. He wrote precisely two thousand words a day, often stopping in midsentence; the next day he completed the sentence, writing until he had two thousand words for the day. Golding once discussed writing in an interview with John Carey. He said he wrote novels because he could not write poetry. He felt he could just manage books: "At any moment it may disappear, between this page and the next. And that's why I write so fast." He kept in his mind a vast store of happenings that he could apply in one situation or another, a kind of metaphor warehouse. "I don't think there is any language but metaphor"; without metaphor, he said, language is like mathematics. Reluctantly, he acknowledged that the novelist is an authority: "In the novel the author is bound to play at God. Because all the time he says, this way, not that. . . . But I would prefer not to think I did, I suppose I have to accept that I do." When interviewer Bernard Dick challenged the source of a quotation in *Pincher Martin,* suggesting that it sounded like the language of Shakespeare's King

Lear, Golding said that he had made up the quotation: "I make up all my quotations." Then Dick suggested that *The Spire* represented the final stage in Golding's evolving style. Golding resisted: "No, I have not yet found a style. I hope I never do." Across the years of his career, Golding's mind churned over what humans should be but never could be and how to write about the dilemma.

FAVORITE PASTIMES

In addition to his writing, Golding took time for traveling. He wrote about his travels in two volumes of essays recording scenes that made strangers and strange places seem familiar. Golding describes trips to Athens and Delphi in Greece and a trip with his family through the Dutch canals in one of his boats, the *Wild Rose*. The boating party came to a long dike which kept the sea from flooding Dutch farmland. In a yacht alongside their boat was a local old-timer. Golding, in his habitual way, struck up a conversation with the old-timer and suggested that the Dutch had perhaps reclaimed enough land from the sea. The old-timer thought differently and quoted an old proverb, "God made the world, but the Dutch made Holland," a job that was still incomplete.

From his days in the navy, Golding never lost his love of sailing or his memories of the English Channel as a sea with stormy weather and dangerous waves. In the summer of 1967, Golding and his family set out across the Channel to explore European canals. During this crossing, a Japanese tanker struck their boat, the *Tenace*, and split it in two; fortunately the tanker returned and rescued the six passengers. Golding's daughter Judy describes the scene after being struck. "Papa found his throat a trifle dry. Calling upon his wife, he requested a glass of water, which my mother fetched, wading thigh deep through the main cabin to get to the galley. . . . I . . . found myself muttering . . . as the *Tenace* wallowed and wallowed—& still the sea came in." In his essay "The English Channel," Golding says, "I have snatched my pleasure from the Channel, knowing full well that every second story about her is someone's tragedy."

Golding publicized another of his hobbies—amateur archaeology—in an essay, "Digging for Pictures," published in *Hot Gates*. Golding liked to explore the area surrounding Stonehenge, which has hidden in its downs and valleys the remains of roads used by ancient people who dwelt there before the Romans came in 55 B.C. "Walk across a newly plowed field and you may pick up a stone spearhead which has not been touched by human hand for 20,000 years . . . [or find] part of a camp lost 3,000 years ago." Though Golding sometimes helped professional archaeologists at scientific digs, he mostly wandered alone, meeting only occasionally a shepherd and his sheep, a man on horseback, a lone hiker, or a herd of cows. He liked his way of pursuing archaeology, which he thought as natural an occupation as gardening is elsewhere; he could imagine coming face to face with a Neanderthal man walking the path he used for his Sunday stroll. "There is a glossy darkness under the turf, and against that background the people of the past play out their actions in technicolor. Sometimes I feel as though I have only to twitch aside the green coverlet of grass to find them there."

LATE NOVELS

Two books fill the space that separates the two major phases of Golding's writing career, the first phase ending with *The Spire* and the second beginning with *Darkness Visible.* The title of the first interim book, *The Pyramid* (1967), comes from Golding's metaphor for science—a pyramid of information that omits the abstract or unquantifiable, concepts like love and the value of music. Set in a fictitious small town near Salisbury called Stilbourne, the novel is episodic: The main character, Oliver, pursues Evie Babbacombe in the first episode, gets involved in a ridiculous production of the Stilbourne Operatic Society in the second, and in the third and final episode visits the grave of his former music teacher, Bounce Dawlish, and reflects on the situation that drove her to insanity. The second interim book, *The Scorpion God* (1971), is a collection of three novellas, unconnected plots unified by an idea of Greek historian Herodotus, the theme that accidents greatly affect history. The title story has a remote setting in which the God-ruler, Great House, is a waning religious power who is overtaken by Liar, the truth teller and incarnation of reason. The second story, "Clonk, Clonk," is set before the biblical fall of Adam in a primeval place called Clonk Clonk, whose inhabitants have a matriarchal society headed by Palm. When one of the men experiences a crisis of loneliness, he changes his name and identity many times hoping to overcome his misery. Women manage situations so that all of the man's changes bring about improvements in his life. The third story, "Envoy Extraordinary," began as a short story before Golding recycled it as a radio play and a three-act play and finally expanded it into a novella. Phanocles, the literal-minded scientist, wants Caesar to adopt his inventions, which will save the world. But Caesar, who can see the future ramifications of the inventions, rejects all but one; he rejects printing, for example, because he can see a future world overrun with worthless books and useless trivia. Caesar rewards Phanocles by sending him away as an ambassador. Both of these books combine satire and allegory.

The major novels of Golding's second phase continue to explore at a deeper level the mystery of evil. *Darkness Visible* (1979), picks up the same theme Golding introduced in *Lord of the Flies* twenty-five years earlier—the darkness of human nature. Golding varies his perspective by putting multiple characters—Matty, Sophy and Toni, Pedigree, and Sim—in metaphorical situations to confront the reader with the dark mysteries of the world. The character Sim draws a conclusion about the human condition: "We're all mad." The next book, *Rites of Passage* (1980), the first book in Golding's sea trilogy, is a lighter novel with a sustained metaphor of a voyage. The reader follows the same characters through three stories of a ship, a microcosm of the larger world. The journey, told through the pages of Talbot's journal, represents rites of passage on personal and historical levels. A poor parson, Colley, also keeps a journal providing a counterpoint to Talbot's. By the end of *Rites of Passage*, Colley is dead, and Talbot has begun to change to be more spiritual, as Colley was.

Golding published three other books before he completed his sea trilogy. In 1982, he published *A Moving Target*, a book of sixteen essays, seven about places and nine about ideas. The year after his 1983 Nobel Prize, Golding published *The Paper Men*, a farce about a writer, Wilfred Barclay, and the scholar who wants to write about him, Assistant Professor Rick L. Tucker. The book has been compared to Samuel Beckett's *Waiting for Godot* because both books have absurd actions and language and both have serious underlying themes. In Golding's next book, *An Egyptian Journal*, he returns to his interest in Egypt, a topic that had preoccupied him since early childhood. *Journal* records Golding's travel experiences in Egypt.

Golding completed his sea trilogy in the late 1980s. *Close Quarters* (1987) continues the story begun in *Rites of Passage.* This second sea novel concerns the ways Colley's story affects Talbot. Talbot confronts himself, and his spiritual outlook becomes more like Colley's. The final book in the trilogy, *Fire Down Below*, written in 1989, completes the transformation of Talbot: He has changed from a man insensitive to the humanity of others to a man so sentimental that he nearly ignores practical matters necessary to save the ship.

HONORS AND PRIZES

For his literary contributions, Golding received many coveted honors in addition to the 1983 Nobel Prize. After publishing *The Spire* in 1964, Golding was made Commander, Order of the British Empire. For *Darkness Visible*, he was awarded the James Tait Black Memorial Prize. Honorary doctorates were conferred by the University of Sussex in 1970 and the University of Kent, University of Bristol, University of Warwick, Oxford University, and the University of Sorbonne, Paris, in 1981. *Rites of Passage* received the prestigious Booker McConnell Prize for the best novel of 1980. Finally, Golding was knighted in 1988.

Golding was presented with the Nobel Prize for literature in Stockholm, Sweden, on December 7, 1983. The presentation speech stressed the paradoxical quality of Golding's stories, at once realistic and mythic. Golding was praised for producing novels in a variety of styles addressing diverse times and places from Egyptian, Greek, and medieval civilizations to the twentieth century. Throughout his career, the speaker noted, Golding maintained the philosophy that corruption arises not from political or economic systems or other social constructs, but from the depth of humans themselves. In his acceptance speech, Golding explained that he is "a universal pessimist but a cosmic optimist"; that is, pessimistic about the notion that rules and science can save the world, but optimistic about the potential that spirituality can help humans reject evil. The writer, he told the audience, must bridge the gap between the scientific mind and the spiritual vision. Humankind may blow up its world or degrade it piece by piece. An alternative is to use the power of language—books, stories, poetry, lectures—to persuade leaders and policy makers to be more careful with nature and the planet. Humans are "children of the stars" growing old with their planet, he concluded.

The Swedish Academy's choice of Golding for the 1983 Nobel Prize brought immediate controversy, beginning within the academy itself when one of its members, Artur Lundkvist, stated publicly that as an author Golding was "decent but hardly of Nobel Prize class," an opinion that prompted Lars Gyllensten to respond that Lundkvist had "the soul of a magpie" and should be disregarded. For a short time, two kinds of criticism spread through Europe and America: that the academy favored geopolitical issues over literary quality and that others, particularly Graham Greene, were more deserving of the prize. Many disparaging opinions came from the American press; *Time* magazine called Golding a "master of textbook despair," and David J. Leigh in *America* said the Golding novels were "unreadable for critics interested in complex structural treatment of political and psychological issues." The criticism, however, was short-lived, and Golding continued to write and publish. Several major critics have since produced studies that give a fuller perspective on Golding's mind and art.

THE ESSENCE OF GOLDING'S CAREER

Golding summed up the essence of his fifty-year writing career in his response to a graduate student who wanted to write a thesis about him because he was a living author. Golding recommended rather that she choose a dead author because "I am a moving target." His goal from the beginning was to know what man is, "whatever man is under the eye of heaven," as he says in "Belief and Creativity," published in *A Moving Target* in 1982. He followed that goal wherever his imagination took him. In the same essay, he says, "A novelist, having gone down from the confusion of daily experience to the supportive multiplicity beneath it and down again to the magical area of his own intuitions will come up to the scaffolding, the supportive machinery of his story." He thought that his novels, the machinery of his stories, should be as different from one another as possible. Moreover, he thought a novelist should create characters in extremity, under stresses, testing them like raw material in a laboratory, making them isolated, obsessed, drowning in a literal sea or in a sea of their own ignorance. He told an audience in Hamburg, Germany, on April 11, 1980:

You may well think that the novelist like the cobbler should stick to his last. I will claim from you the privilege, not of the psychiatrist, philosopher or theologian. I claim the privilege of the story-teller; which is to be mystifying, inconsistent, impenetrable, and anything else he pleases provided he fulfills the prime clause in his unwritten contract and keeps the attention of his audience. This I appear to have done, and it is enough for me.

William Golding died of a heart attack on June 19, 1993, in Perranarworthal, near Falmouth, England, a village in Cornwall, the county where he was born. His obituary in *Contemporary Authors* notes the success of *Lord of the Flies*, which has been reprinted in numerous editions, translated into more than twenty languages, and made into at least two motion pictures.

CHAPTER 1

The Form of *Lord of the Flies*

READINGS ON
LORD OF THE FLIES

Mythical Elements in *Lord of the Flies*

A.D. Fleck

Using *The Golden Bough*, the monumental collection of myths and rituals by James George Frazer as a guide, A.D. Fleck argues that *Lord of the Flies* incorporates images and situations of classic myth. Myths rise out of the fundamental human condition as stories or explanations of how things came to be. Fleck says that read as a myth, *Lord of the Flies* is pessimistic: It implies that humans are inclined toward evil, an inclination that can be seen in the boys' practice of common ancient rites. Fleck suggests that *Lord of the Flies* reminds post–World War II generations that evil indeed lurks beneath the surface of society. A.D. Fleck has lectured in education at the New University of Ulster, where he has been a researcher in language and creative arts.

To turn from *The Golden Bough* to a reading of William Golding's *Lord of the Flies* is to realize how finely the element of myth and ritual has been assimilated into the structure of the novel, and also how different are the conclusions drawn by Frazer[1] and Golding from their narratives. Although the comparative method used in *The Golden Bough*, which takes material from all over the world and from every time and civilization, is out of favour with modern anthropologists, Frazer's work remains a monumental collection of ritual details, folklore, myths and legends together with varying theories as to their origins, a vast quarry of material which has been used by writers as diverse as Freud,[2] Eliot[3] and Golding. . . . The overall tone [of *The Golden Bough*] is one of optimism, for Frazer notes that 'the movement of

1. classicist and anthropologist James George   2. psychoanalyst Sigmund   3. poet T.S.

From A.D. Fleck, "The Golding Bough: Aspects of Myth and Ritual in *The Lord of the Flies*, in *On the Novel*, edited by B.S. Benedikz (London: J.M. Dent, 1971). Copyright 1971 by A.D. Fleck. Reprinted by permission.

higher thought, so far as we can trace it, has on the whole been from magic through religion to science', a faith in 'the progress upward from savagery' which never left him.

In this, Frazer shared the optimism in evolutionary progress of Darwin and Huxley,[4] the early socialists and the tenor of the Victorian age into which he had been born. Golding, who has lived through the horrors of Belsen and Buchenwald, is unable to view man's development in such a light. He writes: 'There were things done during that period from which I still have to avert my mind less I should be physically sick. They were not done by the headhunters of New Guinea or by some primitive tribe in the Amazon. They were done skilfully, coldly, by educated men, doctors, lawyers, by men with a tradition of civilization behind them, to beings of their own kind.' He goes on to stress what he considers to be basic to man's nature, his propensity to evil, evil produced as a bee produces honey.

GOLDING'S VIEW OF HUMANKIND

This, argues Golding, is man's real nature yet it was ignored and hidden by those who urged man's perfectibility and pictured his steady climb up the evolutionary ladder towards 'sweetness and light'. 'I believed then, that man was sick—not exceptional man, but average man. I believed that the condition of man was to be a morally diseased creation. . . .' In theological terms, his pessimistic view of humanity's inherent imperfection is familiar as the fall of man, that 'vast aboriginal calamity', to use Newman's phrase, which sears man's soul, and it is not claimed by Golding that he is saying something startlingly original but something which has to be restated by each generation in its own terms. This, then, is the viewpoint—that each and every one of us is a morally flawed creature—that is put forward in *Lord of the Flies.*

It is for this reason that the novel has been described as a 'fable'. . . . Golding has said '. . . what I would regard as a tremendous compliment to myself would be if someone would substitute the word "myth" for "fable". . . . I do feel fable as being an invented thing on the surface whereas myth is something which comes out from the root of things in the ancient sense of being the key to existence, the whole

4. biologists Charles Darwin and Thomas Huxley

meaning of life, and experience as a whole', and a close examination of the text would seem to support Golding in this, for it is the element of myth which gives *Lord of the Flies* its power to move the reader and to make him start in recognition at the archetypal images and situations which are described in its pages. It is in this connection that a comparison with *The Golden Bough* is illuminating.

Both books are concerned in their different ways with the transition of kingship, with the passing of power and authority from one leader to another. The grim and tragic figure who appears in Frazer's opening chapter is the priest-king who must guard with his life the sanctuary in the grove of Nemi against the arrival of his would-be successor, a runaway slave as he had once been himself who would attempt to break off 'a golden bough', the symbol of his right to challenge the reigning Rex Nemorensis to single combat. . . .

Ostensibly the task which Frazer sets himself is to explain by a wide-ranging collection of comparable customs the meaning of this strange rule of the priest-king. . . . Parallels which Frazer proceeds to draw between the Rex Nemorensis and the protagonists in myths from many times and places emphasize the way in which the whole life of a people, a tribe or a nation, was intimately connected with the health and well-being of their divine king. . . .

POWER SHIFTS FROM RALPH TO JACK

In *Lord of the Flies* it is the rivalry between Ralph and Jack for the leadership of the boys stranded without adult guidance on a tropical island which provides the impetus for the action. From their first meeting we are made aware of a close relationship between these two twelve-year-olds, Ralph who had brought the scattered groups together by blowing the conch shell, and Jack the leader of the choristers who appear out of the midday heat, a dark sinuous creature as they process in their black choir cloaks. Despite Jack's confident claim 'I ought to be chief because I'm chapter chorister and head boy. I can sing C sharp', Ralph is chosen by the vote of the majority of castaways. He is everything a leader should be, handsome with fair hair, good build and a natural ability to command. He also holds the conch which becomes the symbol of order, of fair speech and the rule of reason. Golding describes him as 'old enough, twelve years and a few months, to have lost the prominent tummy of childhood; and not yet old enough for adolescence to have made him awkward. You could see now that he might have made a boxer, as far as width and heaviness of shoulders went, but there was a mildness about his mouth and eyes that proclaimed no devil'.

In marked contrast, Jack is 'tall, thin, and bony; and his hair was red beneath the black cap. His face was crumpled and freckled, and ugly without silliness. Out of this face stared two light blue eyes, frustrated now, and turning, or ready to turn, to anger'. Critic Claire Rosenfield has pointed out that the antithesis between the two boys is strengthened by the way in which Jack and his followers appear out of the darkness and how Jack is dazzled by the sun shining from behind Ralph as they talk. She suggests: 'If Ralph is a projection of man's good impulses from which we derive the authority figures—whether god, king, or father—who establish the necessity for our valid ethical and social action, then Jack becomes an externalisation of the evil instinctual forces of the unconscious.' Golding certainly implies a close relationship between the two, for in the last chapter, as Ralph lies hidden from the boy hunters who are pursuing him to the death, he thinks to himself: 'Then there was the indefinable connection between himself and Jack; who therefore would never let him alone, never'. Ralph and Jack are complementary to each other, one standing for all that is reasonable, the other the man of action who prefers the killing of pigs to talk.

At first they work together sharing the delight of exploring the island—'Eyes shining, mouths open, triumphant, they savoured the right of domination. They were lifted up: were friends'—but soon there are quarrels over the building of shelters and the keeping alight the signal fire on the mountain-top, the older boys preferring the immediate excitement of hunting wild pig to the humdrum activities which Ralph and his closest follower Piggy organize: 'There was the brilliant world of hunting, tactics, fierce exhilaration, skill; and there was the world of longing and baffled common sense'. Golding makes us aware all through the novel of the erosion of Ralph's authority and its passing to Jack. It is Jack and his hunters who provide meat and who involve the others in the mimetic ritual of killing the pig, with its circular dance, its chants, painted faces and symbolic victim.

Eventually Jack gathers to himself all the boys on the island, except Piggy and Ralph, and sits in state on a great log, 'painted and garlanded ... like an idol. There were piles of meat on green leaves near him and fruit, and coconut shells full of drink'. He has become almost a god-king, to be worshipped and offered gifts and who in turn holds the power of life and death. A further stage in his coming into his full inheritance occurs after the raid when Piggy's glasses—the source of fire—are stolen.

> Far off along the bowstave of beach, three figures trotted towards the Castle Rock. They kept away from the forest and down by the water. Occasionally they sang softly; occasionally they turned cartwheels down by the moving streak of phosphorescence. The chief led them, trotting steadily, exulting in his achievement. He was chief now in truth; and he made stabbing motions with his spear. From his left hand dangled Piggy's broken glasses.

The conch, the symbol of order, is ignored by the raiders as it depends for its effectiveness entirely on the recognition by the group of its symbolic function and this recognition has been withdrawn, yet it is only with its destruction 'and the fall through the air of the true, wise friend called Piggy' that all inhibitions are lost by Jack and his followers.

> Suddenly Jack bounded out from the tribe and began screaming wildly.
>
> 'See? See? That's what you'll get. I mean that! There isn't a tribe for you any more! The conch is gone—'
>
> He ran forward stooping. 'I'm chief!'
>
> Viciously with full intention, he hurled his spear at Ralph.

Ralph must die in order that the succession is finally secure, so Jack and his henchman Roger organize the tribe—for we have ceased to regard them as children—to track and kill their former leader. As the Rex Nemorensis must have done two thousand years before, Ralph lurks terrified in the darkness of the forest, without food, lacking sleep, his powers failing, waiting for death and the impaling of his severed head on the stick sharpened at both ends which Roger has prepared. It is only the fortuitous arrival of a naval officer and his men attracted by the smoke of a bush fire which saves Ralph from the fate of the pigs whose heads have already been offered to placate the Beast, the power of evil which the boys feel is on the island.

PIGGY AS A SYMBOL OF REASON

If Ralph and Jack display the forces of attraction and repulsion common to opposite poles, then Piggy, true and faithful unto death, comes to represent the voice of reason which articulates all that Ralph feels but cannot himself express. . . .

Piggy is throughout the novel an outsider, accepted if not fully understood by Ralph but rejected by all the others, yet in his appeal to man's rationality, in his acceptance of science as providing an ultimate answer, he is very much the exemplar of the attitude that everything is susceptible to reason that was popular in the late nineteenth and early twentieth centuries before it was shattered by two world wars. It is the voice also of Sir James Frazer who in the last chapter of *The Golden Bough* describes the way in which 'every great advance of knowledge has extended the sphere of order.'. . .

Golding cannot share Frazer's optimistic view of the nature of science, for science is controlled by a corrupt mankind. It is, after all, as the result of an atomic war that the boys find themselves stranded on the island, and the sign from the adult world that is sought by Piggy and Ralph descends on the island in the form of a dead airman who brings terror to their nights. Nor does their three-fold appeal to reason prevent Piggy and the conch shell being destroyed by the huge rock which Roger levers down upon them. . . .

'I got this to say. You're acting like a crowd of kids.'

The booing rose and died again as Piggy lifted the white magic shell.

'Which is better—to be a pack of painted riggers like you are, or to be sensible like Ralph is?'

A great clamour rose among the savages. Piggy shouted again.

'Which is better—to have rules and agree, or to hunt and kill?'

Again the clamour and again—'Zup!'

Ralph shouted against the noise.

'Which is better, law and rescue, or hunting and breaking things up?'

There can be no doubt in the mind of the reader that Golding's savages would answer with one voice: 'To be painted, to hunt and kill and to break things up, that is what we want.' Man's nature is strongly irrational, he is at the mercy of passions which he only dimly discerns and it is in his hands that the 'golden key that opens many locks in the treasury of nature' has been placed.

SIMON AS A CHRIST FIGURE

The most complex character in *Lord of the Flies* is Simon, 'a skinny, vivid little boy, with a glance coming up from under a hut of straight hair that hung down, black and coarse'. He is also an epileptic, a mystic and the first of Golding's saint figures.

> For reasons it is not necessary to specify, I included a Christ figure in my fable. This is the little boy Simon, solitary, stammering, a lover of mankind, a visionary who reaches commonsense attitudes not by reason but by intuition.

... He alone among the boys feels the real nature of evil on the island, that it is not external but part of their very selves. As the head says in Simon's delirium, 'Fancy thinking the Beast was something you could hunt and kill... You knew, didn't you? I'm part of you? Close, close, close! I'm the reason why it's no go? Why things are what they are?' And when in darkness Simon comes down from the mountain—as Christ after the transfiguration—he is set upon in the frenzy of the boys' ritual dance....

Simon has died in his effort to bring the good news and his flesh is sacrificially eaten after the ritual enactment of the slaying of the Beast. He has become the human substitute, the scapegoat of which Frazer has written:

> ... the employment of a divine man or animal as a scapegoat is especially to be noted, indeed we are here directly concerned with the custom of banishing evils only in so far as these evils are believed to be transferred to a god who is afterwards slain.... On the one hand we have seen that it has been customary to kill a human god in order to save his divine life from being weakened by the inroads of age. On the other hand we have seen that it is customary to have a general expulsion of evils and sins once a year. Now if it occurred to combine these two customs, the result would be the employment of the dying god as scapegoat.

Frazer's 'dying god' has various names: in Western Asia and in Greek lands he was Adonis, in Phrygia Attis, in Egypt Osiris and in Sumeria Tammuz, but whatever the name the myths connected with him had important common features—features which have their echoes in *Lord of the Flies.* In essence, all were vegetation myths which told of the seed which is planted and dies in order that harvest and rebirth will follow, while often the god is killed by a wild boar and the corpse is ceremonially placed in the river or sea. . . .

THE SIGNIFICANCE OF PIGS

Another aspect of the dying god which has already been mentioned is the association in death with pigs and boars— quite appropriately for a vegetation deity as pigs are notorious for the damage they can do to any growing crops. Frazer notes that 'in European folk-lore the pig is the common embodiment of the corn spirit', for example the man who cuts the last stalk of the harvest in certain parts of Germany is said to 'get the sow', in others an effigy of a pig made of straw is carried by the man who gives the last stroke in the threshing, to a neighbouring farm where they have not yet finished, while in Estonia the last sheaf is called the Ryeboar. The pig was held sacred to both Attis and Adonis as they both were reputed to have died while hunting the wild boar.

The relationship between the deity and the pig is not, however, a simple one. . . . Pigs were slain to symbolize the death of the god, yet at the same time were offered as a sacrifice to the god himself [Frazer says:]

> . . . the animal, which at first had been slain in the character of the god, comes to be viewed as a victim offered to the god, on the ground of hostility to the deity; in short the god is sacrificed to himself on the ground that he is his own enemy.

These ambiguities are also present in *Lord of the Flies* in the boys' attitude towards the pigs which they hunt and kill. The animals occur in abundance on Golding's island. . . .

Not only are the pigs the main source of meat for the boys but the ritual associated with the preparation for the hunt and the communal feast assumes religious proportions. The title of Golding's novel, which is synonymous with Beelzebub or the Devil, is applied to the head of the sow which is left impaled upon a stick as an offering to the Beast, as the boys call the force of evil which they sense is on the island. The Beast is seen as a hunter who himself eats pig and it is Jack who makes the suggestion: 'And about the beast. When we kill we'll leave some of the kill for it. Then it won't bother us, maybe'. . . .

The chant which accompanies the mimetic ritual develops from 'Kill the pig! Cut his throat! Bash her in!' to 'Kill the beast! Cut his throat! Spill his blood!' From the beginning of this ritual dance, one of the boys takes the place of a pig in the centre of a circle of hunters. This imitative action is an example of homeopathic magic common to many cultures and described by Frazer as follows:

> ... homeopathic and in general sympathetic magic plays a great part in the measures taken by the rude hunter or fisherman to secure an abundant supply of food. On the principle that like produces like, many things are done by him and his friends in deliberate imitation of the result which he seeks to attain.

So the boys develop their mime from the early days when they play at pig-sticking. . . . It is only a matter of time until the human sacrifice is made, when Simon stumbles into the ring of dancers during the night of the storm and is killed both as pig and Beast.

To the boys the pig therefore becomes both the sacrifice and the god to whom the sacrifice is made, and this is made explicit in the confrontation between Simon and the pig's head. . . .

Simon in his delirium imagines being sucked into the void which is the mouth of the pig. He is being taken within the Beast, and this is later paralleled by the way in which he is swallowed into the circle of boys who are dancing in terror on the beach as the lightning flashes overhead. The ring 'yawned emptily' until Simon comes with his news about the true nature of the Beast, he is taken in, beaten down, torn by teeth and claw until he is spewed forth. He has himself been sacrificed as the Beast and for the Beast. His death is soon to be followed by that of Piggy who is linked by name with the myth of the pig, and who is launched into eternity without even a grunt at the end, his arms and legs twitching on the rock to which he has fallen 'like a pig after it had been killed'. The Beast has claimed his second sacrifice.

THE FUNCTION OF MYTH

In his book *Myths, Dreams and Mysteries*, Mircea Eliade writes:

> A myth always narrates something as having *really happened*, as an event that took place in the plain sense of the term . . . The very fact of *saying* what happened reveals how the thing in question was realised (and this *how* stands equally for *why*). For the act of coming to be is, at the same time, the emergence of a reality and the disclosure of its fundamental structures . . . Myths reveal the structure of reality, and the

multiple modalities of being in the world. That is why they are exemplary models for human behaviour; they disclose the *true* stories, concern themselves with the *realities.*

Myth is not something which is extrinsic to the nature of man but part of the essence of his being, for it provides metaphorical answers to the fundamental questions, 'Why am I here? For what purpose? What is the nature of good and evil? What is my origin and my destiny?' These answers are just as valid as, and in the end perhaps more useful than, the answers provided by science. Golding's novel is also concerned with these fundamental questions, for it places the boys all from respectable middle-class English homes in a demi-paradise in which they burn and destroy and kill.

Their reversion to savagery is made all the more terrible, for Golding does not explain, he simply shows—'the very fact of *saying* what happened reveals *how* the thing in question was realized (and this *how* stands equally for *why*)'. The mythic element in *Lord of the Flies* is intricately connected with what Golding has called 'the terrible disease of being human'. It is not something which has been added in an attempt to give 'significance' to the novel, while the complexity of its integration into the novel's structure would certainly preclude the use of the word 'fable' as an accurate description. Frazer writes:

> It is not our business here to consider what bearing the permanent existence of such a solid layer of savagery beneath the surface of society, and unaffected by the superficial changes of religion and culture, has upon the future of humanity. The dispassionate observer, whose studies have led him to plumb its depths, can hardly regard it otherwise than as a standing menace to civilisation. We seem to move on a thin crust which may at any moment be rent by the subterranean forces slumbering below. From time to time a hollow murmur underground or a sudden spirt of flame into the air tells of what is going on beneath our feet.

It has fallen to the lot of William Golding to remind the postwar generations of this 'thin crust', and to re-emphasize man's mythic inheritance, which is barely concealed by the 'surface of society'. This is what contributes to the density of *Lord of the Flies* as a piece of fiction, and which adds to its relevance in a society which would prefer to ignore the primitive side of man's nature.

Lord of the Flies as Fable

William Golding

In one of a series of lectures given at the University of California at Los Angeles in 1962, William Golding addressed the questions students most commonly ask about *Lord of the Flies*. Golding explained that the novel illustrates that human nature is the source of evil, a view shaped by cruelties he had seen during World War II. He chose the fable form because it afforded him the best opportunity to convey his unpleasant moral, even though the form also imposed limitations. Golding published the lecture in a collection entitled *The Hot Gates and Other Occasional Pieces.*

The fabulist is a moralist. He cannot make a story without a human lesson tucked away in it. Arranging his signs as he does, he reaches, not profundity on many levels, but what you would expect from signs, that is overt significance. By the nature of his craft then, the fabulist is didactic, desires to inculcate a moral lesson. People do not much like moral lessons. The pill has to be sugared, has to be witty or entertaining, or engaging in some way or another. Also, the moralist has to be out of his victim's reach, when the full impact of the lesson strikes him. For the moralist has made an unforgiveable assumption; namely that he knows better than his reader; nor does a good intention save him. If the pill is not sufficiently sugared it will not be swallowed. If the moral is terrible enough he will be regarded as inhuman; and if the edge of his parable cuts deeply enough, he will be crucified. . . .

With all its drawbacks and difficulties, it was this method of presenting the truth as I saw it in fable form which I adopted for the first of my novels which ever got published. The overall intention may be stated simply enough. Before the Second World War I believed in the perfectibility of social man; that a correct structure of society would produce goodwill; and that therefore you could remove all social ills by a reorganization of society. It is possible that today I believe something of the same again; but after the war I did not because I was unable to. I had discovered what one man could do to another. I am not talking of one man killing another with a gun, or dropping a bomb on him or blowing him up or torpedoing him. I am thinking of the vileness beyond all words that went on, year after year, in the totalitarian states. It is bad enough to say that so many Jews were exterminated in this way and that, so many people liquidated—lovely, elegant word—but there were things done during that period from which I still have to avert my mind lest I should be physically sick. They were not done by the headhunters of New Guinea, or by some primitive tribe in the Amazon. They were done, skilfully, coldly, by educated men, doctors, lawyers, by men with a tradition of civilization behind them, to beings of their own kind. . . .

To many of you, this will seem trite, obvious and familiar in theological terms. Man is a fallen being. He is gripped by original sin. His nature is sinful and his state perilous. I accept the theology and admit the triteness; but what is trite is true; and a truism can become more than a truism when it is a belief passionately held. I looked round me for some convenient form in which this thesis might be worked out, and found it in the play of children. I was well situated for this, since at this time I was teaching them. Moreover, I am a son, brother, and father. I have lived for many years with small boys, and understand and know them with awful precision. I decided to take the literary convention of boys on an island, only make them real boys instead of paper cutouts with no life in them; and try to show how the shape of the society they evolved would be conditioned by their diseased, their fallen nature. . . .

One of [England's] faults is to believe that evil is somewhere else and inherent in another nation. My book was to say: you think that now the war is over and an evil thing destroyed, you are safe because you are naturally kind and decent. But I know why the thing rose in Germany. I know it could happen in any country. It could happen here.

TRANSPOSING AN IDEA INTO A STORY

So the boys try to construct a civilization on the island; but it breaks down in blood and terror because the boys are suffering from the terrible disease of being human.

The protagonist was Ralph, the average, rather more than average, man of goodwill and commonsense; the man who makes mistakes because he simply does not understand at first the nature of the disease from which they all suffer. The boys find an earthly paradise, a world, in fact like our world, of boundless wealth, beauty and resource. The boys were below the age of overt sex, for I did not want to complicate the issue with that relative triviality. They did not have to fight for survival, for I did not want a Marxist exegesis.[1] If disaster came, it was not to come through the exploitation of one class by another. It was to rise, simply and solely out of the nature of the brute. The overall picture was to be the tragic lesson that the English have had to learn over a period of one hundred years; that one lot of people is inherently like any other lot of people; and that the only enemy of man is inside him. So the picture I had in my mind of the change to be brought about was exemplified by two pictures of the little boy Ralph. The first is when he discovers he is on a real desert island and delights in the discovery. . . .

This is innocence and hope; but the picture changes and the book is so designed that our last view of Ralph is very different. By the end, he has come to understand the fallen nature of man, and that what stands between him and happiness comes from inside him; a trite lesson as I have said; but one which I believed needed urgently to be driven home. . . .

YEARNING FOR WISDOM

[I took] the children at a moment when mature council and authority might have saved them as on so many occasions we might have saved our own children, might have been saved ourselves. Since a novelist ought not preach overtly in a fable, the situation had to be highlighted by the children having some dim knowledge that wisdom, that commonsense even, is to be found in the world of grownups. They must yearn for it, now they have begun to find the inadequacy of their own powers. I took a moment therefore, when they had tried to hold a council meeting to discuss ways and means but had found that other questions came up—questions which they would sooner have ignored. Finally the meeting breaks down. The children who are retrogressing

1. interpretation as a class struggle

more rapidly have gone off into the wardance with which they fortify their own sense of power and togetherness. It is dark. The few remainder, puzzled, anxious, surrounded by half perceived threats and mysteries; faced with a problem which once looked so simple of solution, the maintenance of a fire on the mountain, but which proved to be too much for them—these few, men of goodwill, are searching for some hope, some power for good, some commonsense.

SIMON'S CHURCH

Simon the saint, as Golding calls him, has his own private place to which he secretly retreats. Golding calls the place a church and describes it with the colors, sounds, and smells of nature.

Simon paused. He looked over his shoulder as Jack had done at the close ways behind him and glanced swiftly round to confirm that he was utterly alone. For a moment his movements were almost furtive. Then he bent down and wormed his way into the centre of the mat. The creepers and the bushes were so close that he left his sweat on them and they pulled together behind him. When he was secure in the middle he was in a little cabin screened off from the open space by a few leaves. He squatted down, parted the leaves and looked out into the clearing. Nothing moved but a pair of gaudy butterflies that danced round each other in the hot air. Holding his breath he cocked a critical ear at the sounds of the island. Evening was advancing toward the island; the sounds of the bright fantastic birds, the bee-sounds, even the crying of the gulls that were returning to their roosts among the square rocks, were fainter. The deep sea breaking miles away on the reef made an undertone less perceptible than the susurration of the blood.

Simon dropped the screen of leaves back into place. The slope of the bars of honey-colored sunlight decreased; they slid up the bushes, passed over the green candle-like buds, moved up toward the canopy, and darkness thickened under the trees. With the fading of the light the riotous colors died and the heat and urgency cooled away. The candle-buds stirred. Their green sepals drew back a little and the white tips of the flowers rose delicately to meet the open air.

'If only they could get a message to us', cried Ralph desperately. 'If only they could send us something grown-up . . . a sign or something.'

What the grown-ups send them is indeed a sign, a sign to fit into the fable; but in the fable sense, that arbitrary sign stands for ... the thing which threatens every child everywhere, the history of blood and intolerance, of ignorance and prejudice, the thing which is dead but won't lie down.... It is perhaps worth noticing that this figure which is dead but won't lie down, falls on the very place where the children are making their one constructive attempt to get themselves helped. It dominates the mountaintop and so prevents them keeping a fire alight there as a signal....

THE LIMITATIONS OF FABLE

Fable, as a method, depends on two things neither of which can be relied on. First the writer has to have a coherent picture of the subject; but if he takes the whole human condition as his subject, his picture is likely to get a little dim at the edges. Next a fable can only be taken as far as the parable, the parallel is exact; and these literary parallels between the fable and the underlying life do not extend to infinity. It is not just that a small scale model cannot be exact in every detail. It is because every sort of life, once referred to, brings up associations of its own within its own limits which may have no significant relationships with the matter under consideration. Thus, the fable is most successful *qua*[2] fable when it works within strict limits....

For reasons it is not necessary to specify, I included a Christ-figure in my fable. This is the little boy Simon, solitary, stammering, a lover of mankind, a visionary, who reaches commonsense attitudes not by reason but by intuition. Of all the boys, he is the only one who feels the need to be alone and goes every now and then into the bushes. Since this book is one that is highly and diversely explicable, you would not believe the various interpretations that have been given of Simon's going into the bushes. But go he does, and prays, as the child Jean Vianney would go, and some other saints—though not many. He is really turning a part of the jungle into a church, not a physical one, perhaps, but a spiritual one. Here there is a scene, when civilization has already begun to break down under the combined pressures of boy-nature and the thing still ducking and bowing on the mountaintop, when the hunters bring before him, without

2. as

knowing he is there, their false god, the pig's head on a stick. It was at this point of imaginative concentration that I found that the pig's head knew Simon was there. In fact the Pig's head delivered something very like a sermon to the boy; the pig's head spoke. I know because I heard it. . . .

REACTION TO *LORD OF THE FLIES*

That is an example of how a fable when it is extended to novel length can bid fair to get out of hand. Fortunately the Lord of the Flies' theology and mine were sufficiently alike to conceal the fact that I was writing at his dictation. I don't think the fable ever got right out of hand; but there are many places I am sure where the fable splits at the seams and I would like to think that if this is so, the splits do not rise from ineptitude or deficiency but from a plenitude of imagination. Faults of excess seem to me more forgivable than faults of coldness, at least in the exercise of craftsmanship.

And then I remind myself that after all, the last lecture on sign, symbol, fable and myth, and this one more particularly on fable, are exercises not in craftsmanship but in analysis. I suspect that art, like experience, is a continuum and if we try to take elements out of that continuum, they cease to be what they were, because they are no longer together. Take these words, then, as efforts to indicate trends and possibilities rather than discrete things. May it not be that at the very moments when I felt the fable to come to its own life before me it may in fact have become something more valuable, so that where I thought it was failing, it was really succeeding? I leave that consideration to the many learned and devoted persons who, in speech and the printed word, have explained to me what the story means. For I have shifted somewhat from the position I held when I wrote the book. I no longer believe that the author has a sort of *patria potestas*[3] over his brainchildren. Once they are printed they have reached their majority and the author has no more authority over them, knows no more about them, perhaps knows less about them than the critic who comes fresh to them, and sees them not as the author hoped they would be, but as what they are.

At least the fable has caught attention, and gone out into the world. The effect on me has been diverse and not wholly

3. native authority, power, control

satisfactory. On the good side it has brought me here, seven thousand miles from home, jet-propelled tho' somewhat jaundiced. It has subjected me to a steady stream of letters. I get letters from schoolmasters who want permission to turn the book into a play so that their classes can act it. I get letters from schoolmasters telling me that they *have* turned the book into a play so that their classes can act it. Now and again I get letters from mothers of boys whose schoolmasters have turned the book into a play so that their classes can act it. I get letters from psychiatrists, psychologists, clergymen—complimentary, I am glad to say; but sometimes tinged with a faint air of indignation that I should seem to know something about human nature without being officially qualified.

And at the last—students. How am I to put this gently and politely? In the first place, I am moved and fulfilled by the fact that anyone of your generation should think a book I have written is significant for you. But this is the standard form of the letters I get from most English speaking parts of the world.

Dear Mr. Golding, I and my friend so and so have read your book *Lord of the Flies* and we think so forth and so forth. However there are some things in it which we are not able to understand. We shall be glad therefore if you will kindly answer the following forty-one questions. A prompt reply would oblige as exams start next week.

Well there it is. I cannot do your homework for you; and it is in some ways a melancholy thought that I have become a school textbook before I am properly dead and buried. To go on being a schoolmaster so that I should have time to write novels was a tactic I employed in the struggle of life. But life, clever life, has got back at me. My first novel ensured that I should be treated for the rest of my days as a schoolmaster only given a longer tether—one that has stretched seven thousand miles.

A Modern Allegory with a Christian Meaning

C.B. Cox

C.B. Cox argues that *Lord of the Flies* succeeds as an allegory because the story is gripping and the style conveys the mystery of nature. Implicit in the novel are the Christian concepts of a universe created with a purpose, humanity as fallen, and sacrifice and redemption as significant acts. Though Cox finds Simon to be a weak character, he also notes that Simon is the one boy who clearly realizes that evil comes from within. C.B. Cox has taught English at the University of Hull and the University of Manchester in England and at the University of California at Berkeley. He is the author of *Joseph Conrad: The Modern Imagination.* With A.E. Dyson, he is the coeditor of several volumes of literary criticism.

William Golding's *Lord of the Flies*, published in 1953, is a retelling in realistic terms of R.M. Ballantyne's *The Coral Island.* A group of boys, shot down during some kind of atomic war, are marooned on an island in the Pacific. In contrast to the boys in Ballantyne's story, who after a number of exciting adventures remember their time on the island as an idyllic interlude, the children in *Lord of the Flies* soon begin to quarrel, and their attempts to create an ordered, just society break down. On one level the story shows how intelligence (Piggy) and common sense (Ralph) will always be overthrown in society by sadism (Roger) and the lure of totalitarianism (Jack). On another, the growth of savagery in the boys demonstrates the power of original sin. Simon, the Christ figure, who tries to tell the children that their fears of a dead parachutist are illusory, is killed in a terrifying tribal dance. The Lord of the Flies is the head of a pig, which Jack puts up on a stick to placate an illusory Beast. As Simon un-

From C.B. Cox, "Lord of the Flies," *Critical Quarterly*, vol. 2, pp. 112-17, 1960. Reprinted by permission of the publisher, Manchester University Press.

derstands, the only dangerous beast, the true Lord of the Flies, is inside the children themselves. Lord of the Flies is the Old Testament name for Beelzebub.

A TWENTIETH CENTURY ALLEGORY

Lord of the Flies is probably the most important novel to be published in this country in the 1950s. A story so explicitly symbolic as this might easily become fanciful and contrived, but Golding has mastered the art of writing a twentieth century allegory. In contrast to the medieval audience, the general reading public today does not believe that correspondences exist between the material and spiritual world, and they do not automatically expect every incident or object to have symbolic importance. No conventions of allegory exist, and the writer cannot introduce colours, animals, flowers or any of the other emblems which were available for the medieval writer. In these circumstances, many novelists have given objects an arbitrary symbolic meaning. . . .

To find an exciting, stimulating plot which is both dramatically credible and capable of allegorical interpretation is exceptionally difficult. The idea of placing boys alone on an island, and letting them work out archetypal patterns of human society, is a brilliant technical device, with a simple coherence which is easily understood by a modern audience. Its success is due in part to the quality of Golding's Christianity. He is neither puritan nor transcendentalist, and his religious faith is based upon his interpretation of experience, rather than upon an unquestioning acceptance of revelation. Although his four novels deal with the depravity of man, he cares deeply about the condition of human life, and shows great compassion for men who suffer and men who sin. His religious sense does not make him turn from life in disgust, but proves to him the dignity and importance of human action. In development of plot, descriptions of island and sea, and treatment of character, he explores actual life to prove dramatically the authenticity of his religious viewpoint.

Lord of the Flies is a gripping story which will appeal to generations of readers. It is easy to despise the power of a good story, and to think of moral implications as an alternative to the obvious devices of surprise, suspense and climax. But to succeed, a good story needs more than sudden deaths, a terrifying chase and an unexpected conclusion. *Lord of the*

Flies includes all these ingredients, but their exceptional force derives from Golding's faith that every detail of human life has a religious significance. This is one reason why he is unique among new writers in the '50s, and why he excels in narrative ability. Typical of the writers of the '50s is an uncertainty about human values, a fundamental doubt about whether life has any importance whatsoever. In contrast, Golding can describe friendship, guilt, pain and horror with a full sense of how deeply meaningful these can be for the individual. The terrible fire which kills the young children, the fear of Ralph as he is pursued across the island, and Piggy's fall to his death on the rocks make us feel, in their vivid detail, Golding's intense conviction that every particular of human life has a profound importance. His children are not juvenile delinquents, but human beings realising for themselves the beauty and horror of life.

CONCRETE DETAILS CREATE VIVID PICTURES

This faith in the importance of our experiences in this world is reflected in Golding's vivid, imaginative style. He has a fresh, delightful response to the mystery of Nature, with its weird beauty and fantastic variety. The conch, which Ralph and Piggy discover in the lagoon and use to call the children to assemblies, is not just a symbol of order. From the beginning Golding does justice to the strange attraction of the shell, with its delicate, embossed pattern, and deep harsh note which echoes back from the pink granite of the mountain. When towards the end of the story the conch is smashed, we feel that sadness which comes when any object of exquisite beauty is broken. The symbolic meaning, that this is the end of the beauty of justice and order, is not forced upon us, but is reflected through our emotional reaction to the object itself.

In this way Golding expresses his passionate interest in both physical and moral life. His narrative style has an unusual lucidity and vitality because he never forgets the concrete in his search for symbolic action:

> Now a great wind blew the rain sideways, cascading the water from the forest trees. On the mountain-top the parachute filled and moved; the figure slid, rose to its feet, spun, swayed down through a vastness of wet air and trod with ungainly feet the tops of the high trees; falling, still falling, it sank towards the beach and the boys rushed screaming into the darkness. The parachute took the figure forward, furrow-

ing the lagoon, and bumped it over the reef and out to sea.

With admirable simplicity this passage conveys a multitude of effects. The incident is part of an exciting story, a surprising climax to the murder of Simon; at the same time the dead parachutist is the 'beast' to the children, a symbol of adult evil, which, by their own act of killing, they have shown to be part of themselves. But the passage achieves its strong emotional impact because it is so firmly grounded in physical awareness. Water cascades from the forest trees, the parachutist 'furrows' the lagoon. These precise words describe with physical immediacy a situation which is real and dramatically poignant. And the picture of the man treading the tops of the high trees recalls the mystery of human life, with its incredible inventions, and yet also makes us feel deep compassion for the ungainly feet, the horror of death.

GOLDING'S POETRY

In William Golding, *Clive Pemberton writes that Golding's language often works on two levels. It conveys both the reality of events and their emotional impact on the reader.*

The question of 'form' is closely related to Golding's literary style, his use of words and phrases which also operate on two levels at once. . . .

It is on this sort of prose that Golding is able to erect his more ambitious effects. The echoes of hymns and psalms and the profusion of light imagery which accompany Simon to his retreat in the forest are intricately and naturally woven into the texture of the narrative. Sometimes a simple word or phrase can take on an extraordinary evocative power. 'Roger ceased to be a pig and became a hunter, so that the centre of the ring *yawned emptily.*' Coming as they do, at the sudden pause and silence just before Simon's arrival at the feast, the words 'yawned emptily' achieve a dreadful hiatus. One is suddenly aware of impending tragedy. Another type of effect is achieved, too, when the frenzied ritual is over, and the stars and the phosphorescent sea fill the scene with brightness and quiet. As the body is borne quietly out to sea, moonbeams, pearls, silver, brightness, marble, effect a kind of transfiguration, by which it is sanctified and the death becomes an elevation. This is essentially the language and the effect of poetry, but it takes off from a prose which is rooted in reality.

The island itself is boat-shaped, and the children typify all mankind on their journey through life. In the opening scenes the island has the glamour of a new-found paradise. With the green shadows from the palms and the forest sliding over his skin, Ralph is overcome by wonder. He lolls in the warm water, looking at the mirages which wrestle with the brilliance of the lagoon. But soon the terrifying fire transforms the island, and illusion gives way to reality. In nightmares the children begin to be afraid that this is not a good island; they become accustomed to the mirages, "and ignored them, just as they ignored the miraculous, throbbing stars". The beauty of the earthly paradise grows stale to their eyes. At the end they leave behind them "the burning wreckage of the island", whose loveliness has been degraded by their presence.

As his attempts to discipline the boys begin to appear hopeless, Ralph, on a search for the illusory beast, sees beyond the lagoon out to open sea:

> The lagoon had protected them from the Pacific: and for some reason only Jack had gone right down to the water on the other side. Now he saw the landsman's view of the swell and it seemed like the breathing of some stupendous creature. Slowly the waters sank among the rocks, revealing pink tables of granite, strange growths of coral, polyp, and weed. Down, down, the waters went, whispering like the wind among the heads of the forest. There was one flat rock there, spread like a table, and the waters sucking down on the four weedy sides made them seem like cliffs. Then the sleeping leviathan breathed out—the waters rose, the weed streamed, and the water boiled over the table rock with a roar. There was no sense of the passage of waves; only this minute-long fall and rise and fall.

This creature becomes a part of Ralph's consciousness, a symbol of a reality he tries to avoid. As he watches the ceaseless, bulging passage of the deep sea waves, the remoteness and infiniteness of the ocean force themselves upon his attention. By the quiet lagoon he can dream of rescue, but the brute obtuseness of the ocean tells him he is helpless. It is significant that the two boys who are killed, Simon and Piggy, are taken back to this infinite ocean.

GOLDING'S CHRISTIAN MEANING

As the waves creep towards the body of Simon beneath the moonlight, the brilliantly realistic description of the advancing tide typifies all the beauty of the world which promises eternal reward to those who suffer:

> Along the shoreward edge of the shallows the advancing
> clearness was full of strange, moonbeam-bodied creatures,
> with fiery eyes. Here and there a larger pebble clung to its
> own air and was covered with a coat of pearls. The tide
> swelled in over the rain-pitted sand and smoothed everything
> with a layer of silver. Now it touched the first of the stains that
> seeped from the broken body and the creatures made a mov-
> ing patch of light as they gathered at the edge. The water rose
> further and dressed Simon's coarse hair with brightness. The
> line of his cheek silvered and the turn of his shoulder became
> sculptured marble. The strange, attendant creatures, with
> their fiery eyes and trailing vapours, busied themselves
> round his head. The body lifted a fraction of an inch from the
> sand and a bubble of air escaped from the mouth with a wet
> plop. Then it turned gently in the water.

Here we become aware of the Christian meaning underlying
the story. For Ralph the sea typifies the insensitivity of the
universe, but this is to see it from only one point of view. The
multitudinous beauties of the tide promise that creation was
not an accident; after our suffering and confusions are over,
a healing power of great beauty will solve all problems. The
advancing waves are like moonbeam-bodied creatures, gently washing the body of Simon free from all stain, and dressing him in pearls, silver and marble in token of the richness
of his love for the other children. Instead of seeking to introduce ancient myths into the modern world, Golding creates
his own, basing his symbols on the actual wonder of life itself. The intricate beauty of the waves is not merely a pleas-
ing arrangement of light and matter, but an incredible manifestation of the wonder of creation, with a valid life in our
consciousness. As Simon's body moves out to open sea
under the delicate yet firm lifting of the tide, it seems impossible that his sacrifice has had no ultimate meaning.

The island, the sea and the sacrifice of Simon all show
Ralph the truth of the human situation. His mind finds the
burden of responsibility too great, and he begins to lose his
power to think coherently: "He found himself understanding
the wearisomeness of this life, where every path was an improvisation and a considerable part of one's waking life was
spent watching one's feet". Jack's return to savagery, taking
all the children with him, is portrayed with frightening realism. The lust for killing grows too strong, and Ralph's inadequate democratic machinery cannot keep it in check. Behind their painted faces, the children can feel a security, a

lack of personal responsibility for the evil they perpetrate, and this desire explains the growth of Jack's prestige. When he tells them they will not dream so much, "they agreed passionately out of the depths of their tormented private lives", and he is amazed by their response. Only the intelligence of Piggy is not tempted by the tribal dances, and his character is presented with great compassion. His fat, asthmatic body is a natural butt for children, and continual mockery has taught him to be humble and to enjoy being noticed even only as a joke. But he has a powerful belief in the importance of civilised order, and gradually Ralph learns to appreciate his value. His death is a poignant reminder of the unjust treatment given by society to so many good men.

SIMON'S VIEW OF REALITY

Simon is perhaps the one weakness in the book. We see his friendship for Ralph, when he touches his hand as they explore the island, and his love of all people when he ministers to the dead body of the parachutist, but alone among the characters his actions at times appear to be motivated not by the dramatic action, but by the symbolic implications of the story. At the beginning, when he withdraws at night from the other children, his motives are left uncertain. But the scene where he confronts the Lord of the Flies is most convincing. In this pig's head covered with flies, he sees "the infinite cynicism of adult life". He has the courage to face the power of evil, and, knowing that the beast is in all of them, he climbs the hill to find out the truth about the dead parachutist.

The whole story moves towards Simon's view of reality. The growth of savagery forces Ralph to make strange speculations about the meaning of human identity. When they hold an assembly at nightfall, he is surprised at the different effect made by the darkness:

> Again he fell into that strange mood of speculation that was so foreign to him. If faces were different when lit from above or below—what was a face? What was anything?

He faces the possibility that there is no absolute perspective to human life, and that all experience may be meaningless. He longs to return to the world of adults, and the irony of this illusion is shown when, after a battle in the skies, the dead parachutist comes down "as a sign from the world of grown-ups". At certain stages of the story, Golding deliberately makes us forget that these are only young children. Their drama and conflict typify the inevitable overthrow of all attempts to impose a permanent civilisation on the instincts of man. The surprising twist of events at the end of the novel is a highly original device to force upon us a new viewpoint. The crazy, sadistic chase to kill Ralph is suddenly revealed to be the work of a semi-circle of little boys, their bodies streaked with coloured clay. But the irony is also directed at the naval officer, who comes to rescue them. His trim cruiser, the submachine gun, his white drill, epaulettes, revolver and row of gilt buttons, are only more sophisticated substitutes for the war-paint and sticks of Jack and his followers. He too is chasing men in order to kill, and the dirty children mock the absurd civilised attempt to hide the power of evil. And so when Ralph weeps for the end of innocence, the darkness of man's heart, and the death of his true, wise friend, Piggy, he weeps for all the human race.

CHAPTER 2

Themes in *Lord of the Flies*

READINGS ON
LORD OF THE FLIES

Several Interpretations of *Lord of the Flies*

Samuel Hynes

Samuel Hynes argues that *Lord of the Flies* is a fable illustrating multiple aspects of evil: Freudian, political, social, and religious. To arrive at these interpretations, Hynes has analyzed the major characters and the novel's central sequence, ending with Simon's murder. By the end of the novel, according to Hynes, the boys have become manifestations of human depravity, indistinguishable from that of adults. Samuel Hynes has taught English at Northwestern University. He is the author of *The Pattern of Hardy's Poetry* and editor of *The Author's Craft and Other Essays by Arnold Bennett.*

Golding has founded *Lord of the Flies* on a number of more or less current conventions. First of all, he has used the science-fiction convention of setting his action in the future, thus substituting the eventually probable for the immediately actual, and protecting his fable from literalistic judgments of details or of credibility. A planeload of boys has been evacuated from an England engaged in some future war fought against "the reds"; after their departure an atomic bomb has fallen on England, and civilization is in ruins. The plane flies south and east, stopping at Gibraltar and Addis Ababa; still farther east—over the Indian Ocean, or perhaps the Pacific, the plane is attacked by an enemy aircraft, the "passenger tube" containing the boys is jettisoned, and the rest of the plane crashes in flames. The boys land unharmed on a desert island.

At this point, a second literary convention enters. The desert island tale shares certain literary qualities with science fiction. Both offer a "what-would-happen-if" situation, in which real experience is simplified in order that certain values and problems may be regarded in isolation. Both tend to simplify human moral issues by externalizing good and evil; both offer occasions for Utopian fantasies. Golding's most immediate source is R.M. Ballantyne's *The Coral Island*, a Victorian boys' book of South Sea adventure, but Ballantyne didn't invent the island dream; that dream began when man first felt the pressures of his civilization enough to think that a life without civilization might be a life without problems.

The relation of Golding's novel to Ballantyne's is nevertheless important enough to pause over. In *The Coral Island*, three English boys called Ralph, Jack, and Peterkin are shipwrecked on a tropical island, meet pirates and cannibals, and conquer all adversities with English fortitude and Christian virtue. We may say that *The Coral Island* is a clumsy moral tale, in which good is defined as being English and Christian and jolly, and especially an English Christian *boy*, and in which evil is unchristian, savage, and adult. The three boys are rational, self-reliant, inventive, and virtuous—in short, they are like no boys that anyone has ever known.

Golding regards *The Coral Island* morality as unrealistic, and therefore not truly moral, and he has used it ironically in his own novel, as a foil for his own version of man's moral nature. . . . One might say that *Lord of the Flies* is a refutation of *The Coral Island*, and that Golding sets about to show us that the devil rises, not out of pirates and cannibals and such alien creatures, but out of the darkness of man's heart. The *Coral Island* attitude exists in the novel—Jack sounds very like Ballantyne's Jack when he says: "After all, we're not savages. We're English; and the English are best at everything." And the naval commander who rescues the boys at the end of the book speaks in the same vein: "I should have thought that a pack of British boys—you're all British aren't you?—would have been able to put up a better show than that—I mean—" But Jack and the commander are wrong; the pack of British boys are in fact cruel and murderous savages who reduce the island to a burning wreckage and destroy the dream of innocence.

THE NOVEL AS A FABLE

The fable of the novel is a fairly simple one. The boys first set out to create a rational society modeled on what "grownups" would do. They establish a government and laws, they provide for food and shelter, and they light a signal fire. But this rational society begins to break down almost at once, under two instinctual pressures—fear and blood lust. The dark unknown that surrounds the children gradually assumes a monstrous identity, and becomes "the beast," to be feared and propitiated; and hunting for food becomes killing. The hunters break away from the society, and create their own primitive, savage, orgiastic tribal society. They kill two of the three rational boys, and are hunting down the third when the adult world intervenes.

This fable, as sketched, is susceptible of several interpretations, and Golding's critics have found it coherent on a number of levels, according to their own preoccupations. Freudians[1] have found in the novel a conscious dramatization of psychological theory: "denied the sustaining and repressing authority of parents, church and state, [the children] form a new culture the development of which reflects that of genuine primitive society, evolving its gods and demons (its myths), its rituals and taboos (its social norms)." The political-minded have been able to read it as "the modern political nightmare," in which rational democracy is destroyed by irrational authoritarianism.... The social-minded have found in it a social allegory, in which life, without civilized restraints, becomes nasty, brutish, and short. And the religious have simply said, in a complacent tone, "Original Sin, of course."

It is, of course, entirely possible that Golding has managed to construct a fable that does express all these ideas of evil, and that what we are dealing with is not alternative interpretations, but simply levels of meaning. The idea of Original Sin, for example, does have political, social, and psychological implications; if it is true that man is inherently prone to evil, then certain conclusions about the structure of his relations to other men would seem to follow. The idea of Original Sin seems, indeed, to be one of the "great commonplaces," one of those ideas which are so central to man's conception of himself that they turn up, in one form or another, in almost any systematic account of human nature. It describes one of perhaps two possible accounts of the nature of human behavior (*The Coral Island* assumes the other one).

---

1. those who accept the basic tenets of the psychoanalytic theories of Sigmund Freud, Austrian physician and founder of psychoanalysis

CHARACTERS AS REPRESENTATIONS OF IDEAS

Since the novel is symbolic, the best approach would seem to be to examine first the "meaning" of each of the major characters, and then to proceed to consider the significance of their interactions. Ralph—in *The Coral Island* the first-person narrator—here provides the most consistent point of view, because he most nearly speaks for us, rational, fallible humankind; Ralph is the man who accepts responsibility that he is not particularly fitted for because he sees that the alternative to responsibility is savagery and moral chaos. He tries to establish and preserve an orderly, rational society; he takes as his totem the conch, making it the symbol of rational, orderly discussion.

Ralph's antagonist is Jack, who represents "the brilliant world of hunting, tactics, fierce exhilaration, skill," as Ralph represents "the world of longing and baffled common-sense." Between them there is an "indefinable connection"; like Cain and Abel,[2] they are antithetical, but intimately linked together—man-the-destroyer confronting man-the-preserver. Jack is the hunter, the boy who becomes a beast of prey (and who uses *kill* as an intransitive verb, an act which is for him an end in itself). He is also the dictator, the authoritarian man-of-power who enters the scene like a drill sergeant, who despises assemblies and the conch, and who becomes in the end an absolute ruler of his tribe. He devises the painted mask of the hunter, behind which a boy may hide, "liberated from shame and self-consciousness," and by painting the boys he turns them into an anonymous mob of murderous savages, "a demented but partly secure society." Jack is the first of the bigger boys to accept "the beast" as possible, and the one who offers the propitiatory sacrifice to it; he is the High Priest of Beelzebub,[3] the Lord of the Flies.

Associated with each of these antagonists is a follower who represents in a more nearly allegorical form the principal value of his leader. Piggy, Ralph's "true, wise friend," is a scientific-minded rationalist, who models his behavior on what he thinks grownups would do, and scorns the other children for "acting like a crowd of kids." He can think better than Ralph, and in a society in which thought was enough he

2. The story of Cain and Abel is recorded in chapter four of Genesis in the Old Testament. Because God praised Abel's offering of a lamb and ignored Cain's offering of "fruit of the ground," Cain killed Abel out of jealousy.   3. an evil spirit, a demon, the devil

would be supremely valuable; but on the island he is ineffectual; he is incapable of action, and is a physical coward. His
totem is his spectacles, and with them he is the fire-bringer;
but when Jack first breaks one lens and then steals the other,
Piggy becomes blind and helpless, a bag of fat. His trust in the
power and wisdom of grownups is itself a sign of his inadequacy; for if the novel makes one point clearly, it is that adults
have no special wisdom, and are engaged in a larger scale,
but equally destructive, version of the savage game that the
hunters play. (When Ralph wishes that the outer world might
"send us something grown-up . . . a sign or something," the
adult world obliges with the dead parachutist, an image of
terror that destroys Ralph's rational society.)

Beside or slightly behind Jack stands Roger, around
whom clings "the hangman's horror." Roger's lust is the lust
for power over living things, the power to destroy life. In the
beginning he is restrained by "the taboo of the old life . . . the
protection of parents and school and policemen and the
law." Jack and the paint of savagery liberate Roger from
these taboos, and "with a sense of delirious abandonment"
he rolls the rock down the cliff, killing Piggy, his opposite.

One character, the most difficult to treat, remains. Simon,
the shy visionary, perceptive but inarticulate, occupies a
central position in the symbolic scheme of the book. It is
Simon who first stammers that perhaps the beast is "only
us," who sees the beast in terms of "mankind's essential illness," and who goes alone to confront *both* beasts, the grin-
ning pig's head and the rotting airman, because, as he says,
"What else is there to do?" Golding has described Simon as
a saint, "someone who voluntarily embraces this beast, goes
. . . and tries to get rid of him and goes to give the good news
to the ordinary bestial man on the beach, and gets killed for
it." He would appear to be, then, at least in Golding's intentions, the embodiment of moral understanding. If this is so,
those symbolic scenes in which he appears will be crucial to
an understanding of the novel.

THE MEANING OF CHARACTERS IN ACTION

I have said that one distinction between Golding's novels and
allegory is that the novels are meaning-in-action, general
truth given narrative or dramatic form by the creative imagination. In considering the meaning of *Lord of the Flies*, one
cannot therefore stop at an examination of character—

SIMON MISTAKEN FOR THE BEAST

At the height of the ritual dance of killing, Simon crawls out of the forest. He has met the beast and come to inform the boys that there is no danger. Mistaken by the littluns as the beast come down from the mountain, the dancers kill Simon and leave him to wash out to sea. This excerpt describes the mob action.

The littluns screamed and blundered about, fleeing from the edge of the forest, and one of them broke the ring of biguns in his terror.

"Him! Him!"

The circle became a horseshoe. A thing was crawling out of the forest. It came darkly, uncertainly. The shrill screaming that rose before the beast was like a pain. The beast stumbled into the horseshoe.

"Kill the beast! Cut his throat! Spill his blood!"

The blue-white scar was constant, the noise unendurable. Simon was crying out something about a dead man on a hill.

"Kill the beast! Cut his throat! Spill his blood! Do him in!"

The sticks fell and the mouth of the new circle crunched and screamed. The beast was on its knees in the centre, its arms folded over its face. It was crying out against the abominable noise something about a body on the hill. The beast struggled forward, broke the ring and fell over the steep edge of the rock to the sand by the water. At once the crowd surged after it, poured down the rock, leapt on to the beast, screamed, struck, bit, tore. There were no words, and no movements but the tearing of teeth and claws.

Then the clouds opened and let down the rain like a waterfall. The water bounded from the mountain-top, tore leaves and branches from the trees, poured like a cold shower over the struggling heap on the sand. Presently the heap broke up and figures staggered away. Only the beast lay still, a few yards from the sea. Even in the rain they could see how small a beast it was; and already its blood was staining the sand.

---

meaning must emerge from character-in-action. In the narrative action certain scenes stand out as crucial, and most of these announce their importance by being overtly symbolic. There is, for example, a series of scenes in which Jack's hunters evolve a ritual dance. On the first occasion, in Chapter 4, a child *pretends* to be the pig, and the hunters *pretend* to beat him. A chapter later the dance has become crueler, "and littluns that had had enough were staggering away, howling." After the next hunt Robert, acting the pig in the dance, squeals with real pain, and the hunters cry "Kill him! Kill him!" After the dance the boys discuss ways of improving the ritual: "'You want a real pig,' said Robert, still caressing his rump, 'because you've got to kill him.'

"'Use a littlun,' said Jack, and everybody laughed." In the final ritual dance, the sacrificial function is acknowledged; the boys' chant is no longer "Kill the pig," but "Kill the *beast!*" and when Simon crawls from the forest, the boys fulfill their ritual sacrifice, and by killing a human being, make themselves beasts ("there were no words, and no movements but the tearing of teeth and claws"). Ironically, they have killed the one person who could have saved them from bestiality, for Simon has seen the figure on the mountaintop, and knows that the beast is "harmless and horrible."

Simon's lonely, voluntary quest for the beast is certainly the symbolic core of the book. The meaning of the book depends on the meaning of the beast, and it is that meaning that Simon sets out to determine. His first act is to withdraw to a place of contemplation, a sunlit space in the midst of the forest. It is to the same place that Jack and his hunters bring the pig's head, and leave it impaled on a stick as a sacrifice to the beast they fear. When they have gone, Simon holds hallucinatory conversation with the Lord of the Flies, Beelzebub, the Lord of Filth and Dung. The head, "with the infinite cynicism of adult life," assures Simon that "everything was a bad business," and advises him to run away, back to the other children, and to abandon his quest. "I'm part of you," it tells him (in words that echo Simon's own "maybe it's only us"), "I'm the reason why it's no go." Simon, apparently epileptic, falls in a fit. But when he wakes, he turns upward, toward the top of the mountain, where the truth lies. He finds the airman, rotting and fly-blown, and tenderly frees the figure from the wind's indignity. Then he sets off, weak and staggering, to tell the other boys that the beast is human, and is murdered by them.

How are we to interpret this sequence? We may say, first of all, that the beast symbolizes the source of evil in human life. Either it is something terrifying and external, which cannot be understood but must simply be lived with (this is Jack's version), or it is a part of man's nature, "only us," in which case it may be understood, and perhaps controlled by reason and rule. Simon understands that man must seek out the meaning of evil ("what else is there to do?"). By seeking, he comes to know it, "harmless and horrible." Thus far the moral point seems orthodox enough. But when he tries to tell his understanding to others, they take *him* for the beast, and destroy him in terror. Another common idea, though a more somber one—men fear the bearers of truth, and will destroy them. This has both political and psychological implications. A "demented but partly secure society" (read: Nazi Germany, or any authoritarian nation) will resist and attempt to destroy anyone who offers to substitute reason and responsible individual action for the irresponsible, unreasoning, *secure* action of the mass. And in psychological terms, the members of a "demented society" may create an irrational, external evil, and in its name commit deeds that as rational men they could not tolerate (the history of modern persecutions offers examples enough); such a society *has* to destroy the man who says, "The evil is in yourselves.". . .

CHILDREN AS ADULTS IN MINIATURE

In discussing the actions of *Lord of the Flies* I have again and again slipped from talking about boys to describing the characters as men, or simply as human beings. It is true that as the action rises to its crises—to the *agon*[4] of Chapter 5, Simon's confrontation with the beast, the murders, the final hunt—we cease to respond to the story as a story about children, and see them simply as *people*, engaged in desperate, destructive actions. Consequently, Golding can achieve a highly dramatic effect at the end of the book by bringing our eyes down, with Ralph's, to a beach-level view of an adult, and then swinging round, to show us Ralph from the adult's point of view. The result is an irony that makes two points. First, we see with sudden clarity that these murderous savages were civilized children; the point is not, I take it, that children are more horrid than we thought (though they are), but rather that the human propensity for evil knows no limits, not even limits of age, and that there is no Age of Innocence (Ralph weeps for the end of innocence, but when did it exist, except as an illusion made of his own ignorance?). Second, there is the adult, large, efficient, confident—the "grown-up" that the children have wished for all along. But

4. a conflict in a work of literature

his words show at once that he is a large, stupid *Coral Island* mentality in a peaked cap, entirely blind to the moral realities of the situation. He may save Ralph's life, but he will not understand. And once he has gathered up the castaways, he will return to his ship, and the grown-up business of hunting men (just as the boys have been hunting Ralph). "And who," asks Golding, "will rescue the adult and his cruiser?"

To return briefly to the question of levels of interpretation: it seems clear that *Lord of the Flies* should be read as a moral novel embodying a conception of human depravity which is compatible with, but not limited to, the Christian doctrine of Original Sin. To call the novel religious is to suggest that its values are more developed, and more affirmative, than in fact they are; Golding makes no reference to Grace, or to Divinity, but only to the darkness of men's hearts, and to the God of Dung and Filth who rules there. Simon is perhaps a saint, and sainthood is a valuable human condition, but there is no sign in the novel that Simon's sainthood has touched any soul but his own. The novel tells us a good deal about evil; but about salvation it is silent.

A Christian Interpretation

Lawrence S. Friedman

Lawrence S. Friedman bases his discussion of *Lord of the Flies* on the idea that Golding is a Christian believer whose novel explores the ramifications of Original Sin, the Christian idea that all humanity bears the residue of Adam's first sin. Golding describes the island as an Eden-like paradise that Jack, the source of evil, enters, overcomes, and destroys. The Christ-figure Simon attempts salvation, but he is no match for the symbolic beast that reigns on the island. Friedman interprets the ending as merely a superficial salvation from the island microcosm, no rescue from the worldwide destruction in which the naval officer is involved. Lawrence S. Friedman has written critically about all of Golding's major works and published *Understanding Cynthia Ozick*, criticism about the works of Jewish writer Cynthia Ozick.

Lord of the Flies opens in Eden.[1] Ralph, fair-haired protagonist, and Piggy, faithful companion and resident intellectual, look about them and pronounce their island good. And so it is, for William Golding has set his young castaways down upon an uninhabited Pacific island as lush as it is remote. Fruit hangs ripe for the picking; fresh water flows abundantly from a convenient mountain; and the tropical climate soon prompts the boys to throw off their clothes. Ralph joyfully stands on his head, an action he will repeat at moments of high emotion. It is easy to forget that the world is at war, and that the plane that carried Ralph, Piggy, and the many other English boys stranded on the island, was shot down by the enemy.

1. the garden of Eden, described in Genesis

Excerpted from *William Golding* by Lawrence S. Friedman. Copyright ©1993 by Lawrence S. Friedman. Reprinted with permission of The Continuum Publishing Company.

As war and plane crash recede from memory, the visible world shrinks to the desert island and its populace of six- to twelve-year-old-boys. Because of the island's fecundity and mild climate the boys are largely exempt from the struggle for food and shelter; because of their youth they are exempt from sexual longing and deprivation; because of their isolation they are exempt from adult constraints. Free to live as they choose, they can act out every boy's dream of romantic adventure until their eventual rescue. *Lord of the Flies* begins, therefore, as a modern retelling of R.M. Ballantyne's Victorian children's classic, *The Coral Island.* Indeed Golding traces his book's genesis to a night when he had finished reading just such an island adventure story to his eldest child. Exasperated by the familiar cutout characters and smug optimism of the original, he conceived of breathing life into a moribund genre by isolating boys on a desert island and showing how they would *really* behave. Ballantyne's shipwrecked boys, somewhat older than Golding's, lead an idyllic life on their remote South Seas island. Tropical nature is benign, the boys' characters conventionally innocent. What evil exists on Coral Island enters in the form of such adult intruders as savage cannibals or pirates. Ballantyne's vision is doubly optimistic: man is inherently good; and good will win out in the end. Like most fairy tales, *The Coral Island* is an amalgam of faith and hope.

On Golding's coral island, Piggy's allusions to atomic war, dead adults, and uncertainty of rescue barely ripple the surface of Ralph's pleasant daydreams. Soon the boys recover a conch from the lagoon. More than a plaything, the conch will become a means of communication, and ultimately a symbol of law and order. Instructed by the wise but ineffectual Piggy, Ralph blows on the conch, thereby summoning the scattered boys. Possession of the conch ensures Ralph's election as chief. Later the assembled boys agree that whoever wishes to speak must raise his hand and request the conch. Cradling the conch in one's hands not only confers instant personal authority but affirms the common desire for an orderly society.

Evil Introduced into the Boys' "Eden"

Read as a social treatise, Golding's first chapter seems to posit notions of fair play and group solidarity familiar to readers of *The Coral Island.* But the same chapter introduces us to Jack Merridew marching at the head of his uniformed column of choirboys. Clad in black and silver and led by an obviously authoritarian figure, the choirboys seem boy Nazis. Frustrated by Ralph's election as chief, Jack barely conceals his anger. The chapter ends with Jack, knife in hand, reflexively hesitating long enough on the downward stroke to allow a trapped piglet to escape. The civilized taboo against bloodletting remains shakily in place as the angry boy settles for slamming his knife into a tree trunk. "Next time," he cries.

It is the exploration of Jack's "next time" that will occupy much of the remainder of *Lord of the Flies.* By fixing incipient evil within Jack, Golding reverses the sanguine premise of nineteenth-century adventure stories that locate evil in the alien or mysterious forces of the outside world. According to Golding his generation's "liberal and naive belief in the perfectibility of man" was exploded by World War II. Hitler's gas chambers revealed man's inherent evil. His followers were not Ballantyne's savage cannibals or desperate pirates whose evil magically dissipated upon their conversion to Christianity. Rather they were products of that very Christian civilization that presumably guarantees their impossibility. Nor does it suffice to accept Ballantyne's implication that his boys' Englishness, like their Christianity, marks them as inevitably good. "We've got to have rules and obey them. After all, we're not savages. We're English, and the English are best at everything. So we've got to do the right things." Coming from Golding's Jack, these words effectively shatter Ballantyne's easy optimism. Conditioned no less by the theology of man's fall than by Nazi atrocities, *Lord of the Flies* traces the spreading stain of man's depravity from its first intimations in Jack to its near-total corruption of the boys and their social order. "I decided," explained Golding, "to take the literary convention of boys on an island, only make them real boys instead of paper cutouts with no life in them; and try to show how the shape of the society they evolved would be conditioned by their diseased, their fallen nature."

Too immature to account for the enemy within, the boys project their irrational fears onto the outside world. The first of these projections takes the shape of a snakelike "beastie," the product of a small boy's nightmare. One side of the boy's face "was blotted out by a mulberry-colored birthmark," the visible sign of the dual nature of fallen man. More by force of personality than by reason, Ralph succeeds in exorcising the monster from the group consciousness. Now the boys struggle to drag logs up the mountain for a signal fire, Ralph and Jack bearing the heaviest log between them. Jack's momentary selflessness combined with the manipulation of the lenses of Piggy's spectacles to start their fire—as well as the very act of fire building itself—signal a resurgence of civilized values. But the fire soon rages out of control; exploding trees and rising creepers reinvoke cries of "Snakes!, Snakes"; and the small boy with the birthmark has mysteriously disappeared. The seed of fear has been planted. Reason has failed to explain the darkness within, and the island paradise begins its fatal transformation into hell.

THE END OF INNOCENCE

Soon Ralph and Jack find communication impossible, the former talking of building shelters, the latter of killing pigs. Increasingly obsessed with his role as hunter, Jack neglects his more important role as keeper of the signal fire. Painting a fierce mask on his face he is "liberated from shame and self-consciousness." Shortly thereafter he and his frenzied followers march along swinging the gutted carcass of a pig from a stake to the incantory chant, "Kill the pig. Cut her throat. Spill her blood." Abandonment to blind ritual has displaced the reasoned discourse governed by the conch. Meanwhile the untended fire has gone out, and a ship has sailed past the island. Lost in blood lust, Jack's thoughts are far from rescue, and he at first barely comprehends Ralph's anger. When he does, he strikes out at the helpless Piggy, shattering one of his lenses. Reason henceforth is half-blind; the fragile link between Ralph and Jack snaps; and ritual singing and dancing resume as the boys gorge themselves on the slaughtered pig. That Ralph and Piggy join in the feast indicates the all-too-human failure to resist the blandishments of mass hysteria.

Killing marks the end of innocence. It is a wiser Ralph who "found himself understanding the wearisomeness of this life where every path was an improvisation and a considerable part of one's waking life was spent watching one's feet... and remembering that first enthusiastic exploration as though it were part of a brighter childhood, he smiled jeeringly." Here at the beginning of the important fifth chapter, "Beast from Water," the regression and initiation themes converge. On the basis of his newfound knowledge, Ralph assembles the boys to discuss such practical matters as sanitation, shelter, and, most crucially, the keeping of the fire. But the tension among the boys is palpable, and Ralph soon confesses, "Things are breaking up. I don't understand why. We began well, we were happy." And he concludes, "Then people started getting frightened." Piggy's theory that life is scientific is countered by new reports of a beast from the sea. Neither Piggy's logic nor Ralph's rules can hold the boys together, and the meeting scatters in confusion. . . .

GOLDING COMMENTS ON ORIGINAL SIN

In an interview conducted on July 10–11, 1985, Oxford professor John Carey asked William Golding to comment on original sin. The answer was published in William Golding: The Man and His Books, *edited by John Carey.*

Original sin—I've been really rather lumbered with original sin . . . I suppose that . . . both by intellect and emotion—intellectually after emotionally—I'm convinced of original sin. That is, I'm convinced of it in the Augustinian way. It is Augustine, isn't it, who was born a twin, and his earliest memory was pushing his twin from his mother's breast? I think that because children are helpless and vulnerable, the most terrible things can be done by children to children. The fact that they are vulnerable, and ignorant of their own nature—can push the twin away from the breast without knowing that they are injuring themselves, without knowing that it's an antisocial action—that is ignorance. And we confuse it with innocence. I do myself. But I still think that the root of our sin is there, in the child. As soon as it has any capacity for acting on the world outside, it will be selfish; and, of course, original sin and selfishness—the words could be interchangeable. . . . You can only learn unselfishness by liking and by loving.

"Beast from the Air" opens with the sign from the world of grown-ups that answers Ralph's desperate cry for help after the breakup of the assembly. Dropping from the air battle high above the island, a dead parachutist settles on the mountaintop where fitful breezes cause him spasmodically to rise and fall. This grotesque "message" recalls the adult savagery that marooned the boys on the island. Moreover, the boys now take the faraway figure for the beast that haunts their dreams. Confronted by its apparent physical reality even Ralph succumbs to fear. The ironic appropriateness of the man-beast foreshadows Jack's growing power and the final unraveling of the social order. Now that the primary task is to kill the beast, Jack assumes command. Promising hunting and feasting he lures more and more boys into his camp. Man regresses from settler to roving hunter, society from democracy to dictatorship.

SIMON'S ENCOUNTER AND DEFEAT

It is at this point, shortly after the collapse of social order under the pressures of inherent evil associated with Jack and irrational fear embodied in the beast from the air, that Golding paints his most startling and powerful scene. Simon, the only boy who feels the need for solitude, returns to his place of contemplation, a leafy shelter concealed by the dense growth of the forest. There he witnesses the butchering of a frantically screaming sow, its gutting and dismemberment, and the erection of its bleeding head on a pole. This head, abandoned by the hunters as a "gift" to the beast, presides over a pile of guts that attracts great swarms of buzzing flies. And the Lord of the Flies speaks: "Fancy thinking the Beast was something you could hunt and kill. You knew didn't you? I'm part of you? Close, close, close! I'm the reason why it's no go? Why things are what they are?" Looking into the vast mouth, Simon sees only a spreading blackness into which he falls in a faint.

As previously noted, Golding has called himself a fabulist and his novel a fable. All fables contain morals; and the moral of *Lord of the Flies* is stated most explicitly in the confrontation between Simon and the pig's head. "I included a Christ-figure in my fable. This is the little boy Simon, solitary, stammering, a lover of mankind, a visionary." Since the Lord of the Flies is Beelzebub, the Judeo-Christian prince of devils, the scene dramatizes the clash between principles of good and evil. To accept the consequences of Golding's symbolism is to recognize the inequality of the struggle between Simon and the head. The Lord of the Flies has invaded Simon's forest sanctuary to preach an age-old sermon: evil lies within man whose nature is inherently depraved. Simon cannot counter this lesson. Engulfed by the spreading blackness of the vast mouth, he is overwhelmed by Beelzebub's power and loses consciousness. While it does not necessarily follow that Christ's message is similarly overpowered by Satan's, the forest scene strongly implies that innocence and good intentions are lost amidst the general ubiquity of evil. That evil cannot be isolated in Jack or in the beast; it is "close, close, close," a part of all of us.

The Simon who awakens from his faint trudges out of the forest "like an old man," stooping under the heavy burden of revelation. Immediately he comes face-to-face with a second awful symbol of human corruption—the rotting body of the downed parachutist. It, too, has been found by the flies; like the pig's head it too has been reduced to a corrupt and hideous parody of life. Releasing the broken figure from the tangled parachute lines that bind it to the rocks, Simon staggers back down the mountain with his news that the beast is harmless. But he stumbles into the frenzied mob of dancing and chanting boys who take him for the beast, fall upon him, and tear him apart.

THE PROCESS TOWARD GOODNESS SEEMS HOPELESS

The ritual murder of Simon is as ironic as it is inevitable. Ironically, he is killed as the beast before he can explain that the beast does not exist. His horrid death refutes his aborted revelation: the beast exists, all right, not where we thought to find it, but within ourselves. Inevitably, we kill our savior who "would set us free from the repetitious nightmare of history." Unable to perceive his truth, we huddle together in the circle of our fear and reenact his ritual murder, as ancient as human history itself. Golding's murderous boys, the products of centuries of Christianity and Western civilization, explode the hope of Christ's sacrifice by repeating the pattern of his crucifixion. Simon's fate underlines the most awful truths about human nature: its blindness, its irrationality, its blood lust.

That the human condition is hopeless is revealed in the fact that even Ralph and Piggy felt the need to join in the "demented but partly secure society" of the hunters just prior to Simon's murder. Later, they console themselves with the excuse that they remained outside the dancing circle. When Ralph recalls the horror of the murder, Piggy first tries to deny its reality. And when Ralph refuses to drop the subject, Piggy shrills again and again that Simon's death was an accident. His desperate rationalizations point to the inability of human reason to cope with the dark reality of human nature. Piggy's excuses are mere frantic attempts to explain away our basest instincts and actions. Their transparent failure to do so marks the limits of the human intellect. Symbolic of the fall of reason is the loss of Piggy's sight. His broken glasses, the means of fire making, are stolen in a raid by Jack and his hunters. As Jack stalks triumphantly off with the glasses dangling from his hand, the reign of savagery is all but sealed.

JACK TRIUMPHS

Jack's victory comes swiftly in the following chapter, "Castle Rock." Again Golding sets up a contest between principles of good and evil. But this time the outcome is a foregone conclusion. The pack of painted savages who blindly murdered Simon has by now abandoned all restraints. Personified by Roger, Jack's fanatical self-appointed "executioner," the hunters turn viciously against Ralph and Piggy and the twins Sam and Eric, the last four remnants of an orderly society. From high atop a cliff Roger pushes a great rock that, gathering momentum, strikes Piggy, killing the fat boy and shattering the conch. Although the conch has long since lost the power to invoke order, its explosion signals the final triumph of lawlessness. Screaming wildly, "I'm chief," Jack hurls his spear at Ralph, inflicting a flesh wound, and forcing the former chief to run frantically for his life.

"Cry of the Hunters," the novel's concluding chapter, marks the final degenerative stage in Golding's fable of man's fall. Ralph's pursuers, freed by Piggy's murder from the faint restraint of reason, have reduced Ralph to their quarry. As the savage pack closes in, the sad lesson of the hunt is inescapable: not that the boys are dehumanized, but that they are all too human. Man's basic instinct is to kill; and the depth of his depravity is measured by the urge to kill his own species. Not only does the metaphor of the hunt complete Golding's definition of the human animal, but it forges a link to analogous hunts in Greek drama that loom in the background of *Lord of the Flies*.

Golding has often acknowledged the formative influence of the ancients. Together with the biblical version of man's fate expressed in the doctrine of original sin, Greek drama fleshes out the myth of the fall. If it is true that a writer's forebears surface most apparently in his early work, then the final hunt of *Lord of the Flies* is second only to Simon's "passion" in fixing the origins of Golding's most cherished ideas. While it is true that Simon's confrontation with the pig's head and his subsequent martyrdom are couched primarily in Christian terms, the Greek influence is also apparent. The pig's head is at once the Judeo-Christian Beelzebub and the king of the Olympian gods. . . .

Man's blood lust is balanced by his reverence for the gods, a view shared by Golding: "As far back as we can go in history we find that the two signs of man are a capacity to kill and a belief in God." Human fear and guilt are perverse affirmations of the gods' existence and therefore find favor with the gods. . . . For Golding, the Christian believer, man is lost without God. The absence of prayer, even among fearful young choirboys, is one of the darkest aspects of *Lord of the Flies*. . . .

SUPERFICIAL SALVATION BY THE NAVAL OFFICER

Against the backdrop of the flaming island, a hell that once was Eden, the savage tribe pursues Ralph until, stumbling over a root, the frantic boy sprawls helplessly in the sand. Staggering to his feet, flinching at the anticipated last onslaught, Ralph looks up into the astonished face of a British naval officer. Ralph's miraculous salvation completes the drama of his initiation as, in a shattering epiphany, he weeps "for the end of innocence, the darkness of man's heart, and the fall through the air of the true wise friend called Piggy.". . .

Golding's spiffy naval officer is, however, no god. Nor does he represent a higher morality. Confronted by the ragtag melee, he can only wonder that English boys hadn't put up a better show, and mistakes their savage hunt for fun and games à la *The Coral Island*. While he cannot know the events preceding his arrival, his comments betray the same ignorance of human nature that contributed to the boys' undoing. Commanding his cruiser, the officer will direct a maritime search-and-destroy mission identical to the island hunt. *Lord of the Flies* ends with the officer gazing at the cruiser, preparing to reenact the age-old saga of man's inhumanity to man. . . .

Ralph can only weep for the loss of innocence from the world; he shows no particular signs of coping with his newfound knowledge. To understand one's nature is not to alter it. Morally diseased, mired in original sin, fallen man can rise only by the apparently impossible means of transcending his very nature. In man's apparent inability to re-create himself lies the tragedy of *Lord of the Flies.* The futility of Simon's sacrificial death, the failure of adult morality, and the final absence of God create the spiritual vacuum of Golding's novel. . . . For Golding, God's absence leads only to despair and human freedom is but license. "The theme of *Lord of the Flies* is grief, sheer grief, grief, grief."

The Meaning of the Beast

James R. Baker

James R. Baker argues that the moral failure of the schoolboys in *Lord of the Flies* results from their failure to confront the darkness within their own natures. Baker analyzes the ways Golding drew on both Christian and Greek literature to develop his own myth about the existence of evil. Golding's major characters err by trying to use reason to control their nature, Baker explains. Only Simon, a saint, sees the truth, but like all saints, he is killed because his message is unbearable to others. In its broadest context, Baker argues, the symbolic beast is always reborn when humans deny their potential for moral wrongdoing. James R. Baker has taught English in Southern California. He is the cofounder of the *Faulkner Studies* and *Twentieth Century Literature*.

If there is any literary precedent for the image of man contained in Golding's fable, it is obviously not to be discovered within the framework of a tradition that embraces *Robinson Crusoe* and *Swiss Family Robinson* and that includes also the island episodes in Conrad's[1] novels. . . .

THE INFLUENCE OF CLASSICAL LITERATURE

Quite removed from this tradition (which Golding mocks in nearly everything he has written) is the directly acknowledged influence of classical Greek literature. Within this designation, though Golding's critics have ignored it, is the acknowledged admiration for Euripides. Among the plays of Euripides it is *The Bacchae* that Golding, like his Mamillius of *The Brass Butterfly*, obviously knows by heart. The

---

1. novelist Joseph

tragedy is a bitter allegory on the degeneration of society, and it contains a basic parable which informed much of Golding's work. It is clearly pertinent in *Lord of the Flies.* . . .

The Bacchae, however, is more than an expression of disillusionment with a failing democracy. Its aim is precisely what Golding has declared to be his own: "to trace the defects of society back to the defects of human nature," and so to account for the failure of rational man who invariably undertakes the blind ritual-hunt in which he seeks to kill the threatening "beast" within his own being.

The Bacchae is based on a legend of Dionysus wherein the god (a son of Zeus and the mortal Semele, daughter of Cadmus) descends upon Thebes in great wrath, determined to take revenge upon the young king, Pentheus, who has denied him recognition and prohibited his worship. Dionysus wins the daughters of Cadmus as his devotees; and, through his power of enchantment, he decrees that Agave, mother of Pentheus, shall lead the group in frenzied celebrations. Pentheus bluntly opposes the god and tries by every means to preserve order against the rising tide of madness in his kingdom. The folly of his proud resistance is shown in the total defeat of all his efforts: the bacchantes trample on his rules and edicts; in wild marches through the land they wreck everything in their path. Thus prepared for his vengeance, Dionysus casts a spell over Pentheus. With his judgment weakened and his identity obscured by dressing as a woman, the humiliated prince sets out to spy upon the orgies. In the excitement of their rituals the bacchantes live in a world of illusion, and all that falls within their sight undergoes a metamorphosis which brings it into accord with the natural images of their worship. When Pentheus is seen, he is taken for a lion. Led by Agave, the blind victims of the god tear the king limb from limb. The final punishment of those who denied the god of nature is to render them conscious of their awful crimes and to cast them out from their homeland as guilt-stricken exiles and wanderers upon the earth.

For most modern readers the chief obstacle in the way of proper understanding of *The Bacchae*, and therefore of Golding's use of it, is the popular notion that Dionysus is nothing more than a charming god of wine. . . . [According to E.R. Dodds in *Euripides Bacchae*] the god was more important and "much more dangerous": he was "the principle of animal life . . . the hunted and the hunter—the unrestrained potency which man envies in the beasts and seeks to assimilate." Thus the intention and chief effect of the bacchanal[2] is "to liberate the instinctive life in man from the bondage imposed upon it by reason and social custom.". . .

Dionysus was worshiped in various animal incarnations (snake, bull, lion, boar), whatever form was appropriate to place; and all of these incarnations were symbolic of the impulses he evoked in his worshipers. In *The Bacchae* a leader of the bacchanal summons him with the incantation, "O God, Beast, Mystery, come!" Agave's attack upon the "lion" (her own son) conforms to the codes of Dionysic ritual: like other gods, this one is slain and devoured, his devotees sustained by his flesh and blood. The terrible error of the bacchantes is a punishment brought upon the proud Greeks by the lord of beasts: "To resist Dionysus is to repress the elemental in one's own nature; the punishment is the sudden collapse of the inward [dikes] when the elemental breaks through perforce and civilization vanishes," [according to Dodds].

THE SCHOOLBOYS' ERRORS

This same lesson in humility is meted out to the schoolboys of *Lord of the Flies*. In their innocent pride they attempt to impose a rational order or pattern upon the vital chaos of their own nature, and so they commit the error and "sin" of Pentheus, the "man of many sorrows." The penalties (as in the play) are bloodshed, guilt, utter defeat of reason. Finally, they stand before the officer, "A semicircle of little boys, their bodies streaked with colored clay, sharp sticks in their hands." Facing that purblind[3] commander (with his revolver and peaked cap), Ralph cries "for the end of innocence, the darkness of man's heart"; and the tribe of vicious hunters joins him in spontaneous choral lament. But even Ralph could not trace the arc of their descent, could not explain why it's no go, why things are as they are. For in the course of events he was at times among the hunters, one of them; and he grieves in part for the appalling ambiguities he has discovered in his own being. In this moment of "tragic knowledge" he remembers those strange interims of blindness and despair when a "shutter" clicked down over his mind and left him at the mercy of his own dark heart. In Ralph's experience, then, the essence of the fable is spelled

2. a celebration honoring Dionysus   3. slow in understanding

out: he suffers the dialectic[4] we must all endure, and his failure to resolve it as we would wish demonstrates the limitations which have always plagued our species.

In the first hours on the island Ralph sports untroubled in the twilight of childhood and innocence, but after he sounds the conch he must confront the forces he has summoned to the granite platform beside the sunny lagoon. During that first assembly he seems to arbitrate with the grace of a young god (his natural bearing is dignified, princely); and, for the time being, a balance is maintained. The difficulties begin with the dream revelation of the child distinguished by the birthmark. The boy tells of a snakelike monster prowling the woods by night, and at this moment the seed of fear is planted. Out of it will grow the mythic beast destined to become lord of the island. There is a plague of haunting dreams, and these constitute the first symptoms of the irrational fear which is "mankind's essential illness."

In the chapter entitled "Beast from Water" the parliamentary debate becomes a blatant allegory in which each spokesman caricatures the position he defends. Piggy (the voice of reason) leads with the statement that "life is scientific," and adds the usual utopian promises. . . . Maurice interjects to voice the doubt which curses them all: "I don't believe in the beast of course. As Piggy says, life's scientific, but we don't know, do we? Not certainly."

THE FAILURE OF SIMON'S WARNING

Then Simon (the inarticulate seer) rises to utter the truth in garbled ineffective phrases: there *is* a beast, but "it's only us." As always, his saving words are misunderstood, and the prophet shrinks away in confusion. Amid the speculation that Simon means some kind of ghost, there is a silent show of hands for ghosts as Piggy breaks in with angry rhetorical questions: "What are we? Humans? Or animals? Or savages?" Taking his cue, Jack (savagery *in excelsis*) leaps to his feet and leads all but the "three blind mice" (Ralph, Piggy, and Simon) into a mad jig of release down the darkening beach. The parliamentarians naïvely contrast their failure with the supposed efficiency of adults; and Ralph, in despair, asks for a sign from that ruined world.

In "Beast from Air" the sign, a dead man in a parachute,

---

4. the contradiction between two conflicting forces

is sent down from the grownups, and the collapse of order foreshadowed in the allegorical parliament comes on with surprising speed. Ralph himself looks into the face of the enthroned tyrant on the mountain, and from that moment his young intelligence is crippled by fear. He confirms the reality of the beast, insuring Jack's spectacular rise to absolute power. Yet the ease with which Jack establishes his Dionysian regime is hardly unaccountable. From its very first appearance, the black-caped choir, vaguely evil in its military *esprit*,[5] emerged ominously from a mirage and marched down upon the minority forces assembled on the platform. Except for Simon, pressed into service and out of step with the common rhythm, the choir is composed of servitors bound by the rituals and the mysteries of group consciousness. They share in that communion, and there is no real "conversion" or transfer of allegiance from good to evil when the chorus, ostensibly Christian, becomes the tribe of hunters. The god they serve inhabits their own being. If they turn with relief from the burdens and responsibilities of the platform, it is because they cannot transcend the limitations of their own nature. . . .

SIMON CONFRONTS THE BEAST

It is Simon who witnesses [the great god's] coming and hears his words of wrath. In the thick undergrowth of the forest the boy discovers a refuge from the war of words. His shelter of leaves is a place of contemplation, a sequestered temple scented and lighted by the white flowers of the night-blooming candle-nut tree. There, in secret, he meditates on the lucid but somehow oversimple logic of Piggy and Ralph and on the venal[6] emotion of Jack's challenges to their authority. There, in the infernal glare of the afternoon sun, he sees the killing of the sow by the hunters and the erection of the pig's head on the sharpened stick. These acts signify not only the final release from the blood taboo but also obeisance to the mystery and god who has come to be lord of the island world. In the hours of one powerfully symbolic afternoon, Simon sees the perennial fall which is the central reality of our history: the defeat of reason and the release of Dionysian madness in souls wounded by fear.

---

5. liveliness in spirit, enthusiasm   6. capable of betraying honor, duty, or scruples; corruptible

Awed by the hideousness of the dripping head—an image of the hunters' own nature—the apprentice bacchantes suddenly run away; but Simon's gaze is "held by that ancient, inescapable recognition"—an incarnation of the beast or devil born again and again out of the human heart. Before he loses consciousness, the epileptic visionary "hears" the truth which is inaccessible to the illusion-bound rationalist and to the unconscious or irrational man alike. "'Fancy thinking the Beast was something you could hunt and kill!' said the head. For a moment or two the forest and all the other dimly appreciated places echoed with the parody of laughter. 'You knew, didn't you? I'm part of you? Close, close, close! I'm the reason why it's no go? Why things are as they are?'" When Simon recovers from this trauma of revelation, he finds on the mountaintop that the "beast" is only a man. Like the pig itself, the dead man in the chute is fly-blown, corrupt; he is an obscene image of the evil that has triumphed in the adult world as well. Tenderly the boy releases the lines so that the body can descend to earth, but the fallen man does not descend. After Simon's death, when the truth is once more lost, the figure rises, moves over the terrified tribe on the beach, and finally out to sea—a tyrannous ghost (history itself) which haunts and curses every social order.

In his martyrdom Simon meets the fate of all saints. The truth he brings would set us free from the repetitious nightmare of history, but we are, by nature, incapable of perceiving that truth. Demented by fears our intelligence cannot control, we are "at once heroic and sick.". . .

Simon, the saintly one, is blessed and cursed by those unique intuitions which threaten the ritual of the tribe. In whatever culture he appears, the saint is doomed by his insights. There is a vital, if obvious, irony to be observed in the fact that the lost children of Golding's fable are of Christian heritage; but, when they blindly kill their savior, they reenact not only an ancient tragedy but a universal one because it has its true source in the defects of the species.

THE NATURE OF THE BEAST

The beast, too, is as old as his maker and has assumed many names, though of course his character must remain quite consistent. The particular beast who speaks to Simon is much like his namesake, Beelzebub. A prince of demons of Assyrian or Hebrew descent, but later appropriated by

Christians, he is a lord of flies, an idol for unclean beings. He is what all devils are: merely an embodiment of the lusts and cruelties which possess his worshipers and of peculiar power among the Philistines, the unenlightened, fearful herd. He shares some kinship with Dionysus, for his powers and effects are much the same. In *The Bacchae* Dionysus is shown "as the source of ecstasies and disasters, as the enemy of intellect and the defense of man against his isolation, as a power that can make him feel like a god while acting like a beast." As such, he is "a god whom all can recognize," [according to R.P. Winnington-Ingram in *Euripides and Dionysus: An Interpretation of the Bacchae*].

Nor is it difficult to recognize the island on which Golding's innocents are set down as a natural paradise, an uncorrupted Eden offering all the lush abundance of the primal earth. But it is lost with the first rumors of the "snake-thing," because he is the ancient, inescapable presence who insures a repetition of the fall. If this fall from grace is indeed the "perennial myth" that Golding explores in all his work, it does not seem that he has found in Genesis a metaphor capable of illuminating the full range of his theme. In *The Bacchae* Golding the classicist found another version of the fall of man, and it is clearly more useful to him than its Biblical counterpart. . . .

To resist Dionysus is to resist nature itself, and this attempt to transcend the laws of creation brings down upon us the punishment of the god. Further, the ritual hunt of *The Bacchae* provides something else not found in the Biblical account of the fall. The hunt on Golding's island emerges spontaneously out of childish play, but it comes to serve as a key to the psychology underlying adult conflicts and, of course, as an effective symbol for the bloody game we have played throughout our history. This is not to say that Biblical metaphor is unimportant in *Lord of the Flies*, or in the later works, but that it forms only a part of the larger mythic frame in which Golding sees the nature and destiny of man.

Unfortunately, the critics have concentrated all too much on Golding's debts to Christian sources, with the result that he is now popularly regarded as a rigid Christian moralist. This is a false image. The emphasis of the critics has obscured Golding's fundamental realism and made it difficult to recognize that he satirizes both the Christian and the rationalist point of view. In *Lord of the Flies*, for example, the much discussed last chapter offers none of the traditional comforts of Christian orthodoxy. A fable, by virtue of its far-reaching suggestions, touches upon a dimension that most fiction does not—the dimension of prophecy. With the appearance of the naval officer, it is no longer possible to accept the evolution of the island society as an isolated failure. The events we have witnessed constitute a picture of realities which obtain in the world at large. There, too, a legendary beast has emerged from the dark wood, come from the sea, or fallen from the sky; and men have gathered for the communion of the hunt. . . .

The childish hope of rescue perishes as the beast-man comes to the shore, for he bears in his nature the bitter promise that things will remain as they are—and as they have been since his first appearance ages and ages ago.

The rebirth of evil is made certain by the fatal defects inherent in human nature, and the haunted island we occupy must always be a fortress on which enchanted hunters pursue the beast. There is no rescue. The making of history and the making of myth are finally the selfsame process—an old one in which the soul makes its own place, its own reality.

Lord of the Flies Is Impossible to Categorize

Irving Malin

Irving Malin argues that in *Lord of the Flies* the outer world of science and material objects never merges with the elusive inner world of self. Malin arrives at this meaning by testing various interpretations. For example, Golding's novel is like poetry in many ways, but, unlike poetry, the inner and outer worlds remain separated. Golding's major characters appear to symbolize the elements of earth, air, fire, and water, but Golding does not make the correspondences equal. Malin concludes that Golding clearly creates a distorted place where elements do not or cannot come together. Irving Malin has taught English at City College of New York. He is the author of *New American Gothic, Jews and Americans*, and a book on American novelist William Faulkner.

William Golding refuses to deal with conventional themes, characters, or situations. He avoids neat categories. He irritates us so much that we are tempted to label and forget him. Some critics have already done this (with great respect). Frederick R. Karl writes that Golding's "eccentric themes, unfortunately, rarely convey the sense of balance and ripeness that indicate literary maturity...." James Gindin objects to his self-defeating "gimmicks." V.S. Pritchett calls his last two novels, *Free Fall* and *The Spire*, "obscure, strained, and monotonous." But Golding remains a problem.

Perhaps we can respond freshly to his works—are they novels or fables?—only if we question our usual critical assumptions. Do novels have to deal with social issues? What is artistic maturity? Is language as powerful as gesture? Such radical questions are avoided by the three critics mentioned

From "The Elements of William Golding" by Irving Malin, in *Contemporary British Novelists*, edited by Charles Shapiro. Copyright ©1965 by Southern Illinois University Press. Reprinted by permission of Southern Illinois University Press.

above, who accept vague definitions of novelistic "reality." Golding asks himself these very questions—in his novels. He presents the constant battle between primitive levels of response and deceptive consciousness, the beast and the human. Because he tends to view this conflict within one being, he does not portray complex social character. His heroes are more aware of elemental nature than of social adaptation. They are flat and stylized; they do not seem to belong in novels (at least the ones we are used to).

Golding's psychology shapes his novels. He wants to give us the "poetry of disorder" (Richard Chase's phrase), not the science of order. But the very words he uses are logical; they discipline elemental nature, destroying some of its violent, sudden beauty. How can he express his *vision* of our primitivism when this very expression mutilates it? Golding's strange novels are, by their very nature, suicidal because they cannot capture those ambiguous gestures which are below (or above?) language. To claim that he does not know what he is doing; to assert that he is unnecessarily eccentric—such statements assume the incompetence of Golding, whereas they confirm the limitations of his critics.

But are Golding's views so unusual? If we look at Gaston Bachelard's criticism, for example, we see that he also recognizes the need for elemental return. He believes that science—any logical pattern—cannot comprehend reality: it is seduced often unwittingly, by what is "out there"; it disregards the elemental nature of life. "Fire is no longer a reality for science" because it—like earth, air, or water—becomes a simple datum of experience, not a complex object of reverie. Poetry, on the other hand, refuses to settle for deceptive measurement: it does not assume that "out there" can be separated from "in here"; it constructs an intuitive *field* of subject and object, reverie and element. *Golding's novels question and construct this same field.*

Lord of the Flies (1954) has been frequently discussed in the last few years in terms of Original Sin, the Freudian Trinity,[1] and the Parody of *The Coral Island*.[2] But as Bern Oldsey and Stanley Weintraub have pointed out, it refuses to be conveniently categorized. They believe that the four boys—Simon, Piggy, Ralph, and Jack—are "endlessly" suggestive. Perhaps their most significant statement (for our purpose) is

1. the id, the ego, and the superego   2. a children's story by R.M. Ballantyne

the following:

> the major characters . . . are usually identified in the book with certain imagery and talismanic objects: Jack with blood and dung, with the mask of primitive tribalism (imagistically he is in league with the Lord of the Flies); Piggy with pig's meat (his physical sloth and appetite and eventual sacrifice), with his glasses that represent intellect and science (though they could hardly coax the sun into making fire);

RALPH SURVEYS THE ISLAND

Golding introduces the readers to the island setting through Ralph's eyes—"visible" heat, coconut shells like skulls, palms as a "green roof"—and gives Ralph a variety of perspectives —standing, upside down, sitting, one eye shut, underwater.

Within the irregular arc of coral the lagoon was still as a mountain lake—blue of all shades and shadowy green and purple. The beach between the palm terrace and the water was a thin stick, endless apparently, for to Ralph's left the perspectives of palm and beach and water drew to a point at infinity; and always, almost visible, was the heat. . . .

• • • • •

Then he leapt back on the terrace, pulled off his shirt, and stood there among the skull-like coconuts with green shadows from the palms and the forest sliding over his skin. . . .

• • • • •

He patted the palm trunk softly, and, forced at last to believe in the reality of the island, laughed delightedly again and stood on his head. He turned neatly on to his feet, jumped down to the beach, knelt and swept a double armful of sand into a pile against his chest. Then he sat back and looked at the water with bright, excited eyes. . . .

• • • • •

The palms that still stood made a green roof, covered on the underside with a quivering tangle of reflections from the lagoon. Ralph hauled himself on to this platform, noted the coolness and shade, shut one eye, and decided that the shadows on his body were really green. . . .

• • • • •

But the island ran true to form and the incredible pool, which clearly was only invaded by the sea at high tide, was so deep at one end as to be dark green. Ralph inspected the whole thirty yards carefully and then plunged in. The water was warmer than his blood and he might have been swimming in a huge bath.

Ralph with the conch and the signal fire, with comeliness
and the call to duty, with communal hope. (*College English*,
November, 1963)

Lord of the Flies is more than an adventure story or allegory
because of this very insistence upon "odd" objects. By placing his boys upon a mysterious island—where is it?—Golding forces them to explore the landscape. Earth, air, fire,
water—these shape and hold the meanings of existence.

FOUR ELEMENTS: FOUR BOYS

The four elements—the four boys. How convenient it would
be if Golding were to equate them! Piggy and fire? Jack and
earth? Simon and air? Ralph and water? But we feel cheated.
There is no *one* element for each boy because Golding realizes that even "primitive life" remains mysterious. There is no
doubt, however, that just as the Elizabethans employed the
four humours—based on the four elements—he associates
personality and element. This association is more lasting than
the incantation of old names. The four boys constantly touch
the elements, whether or not they realize they do. Because
they are bound to different elements (in different combina-
tions) they battle one another. And they torment themselves in
their desire to rule (or be ruled by) only one element.

Throughout the novel Golding refers to the illusive quality of the island. Simon, for example, sees "a pearly stillness,
so that what was real seemed illusive and without definition." Piggy peers "anxiously into the luminous veil that
hung between him and the world." Jack peers "into what to
him was almost complete darkness" when he first arrives on
the beach. Because the elements are shadowy and ambiguous (and threatening?), they defy the vision of all the boys,
including Simon and Piggy. Thus we have a completely
ironic situation. The boys are forced to return to the elements—to exist "originally"—but they are so deceived by
magical qualities that they cannot clearly judge their experience. Although many critics have complained about the
gimmick at the end of the novel—the boys are saved; the officer doesn't "understand" the violence which has oc-
curred—it is justified because it is another "appearance."
The officer allows his "eyes to rest on the trim cruiser in the
distance," but we doubt that he can see it or the water with
full knowledge.

Lord of the Flies is therefore a novel of faulty vision. Can the boys ever see the elements? Are the elements really there? Is a marriage between elements and consciousness possible? The novel is not about Evil, Innocence, or Free Will; it goes beyond (or under) these abstractions by questioning the very ability to formulate them.

Look at any crucial scene. There is an abundance of descriptive details—the elements are "exaggerated" because they are all that the boys possess—but these details are blurred in one way or another. The result is, paradoxically, a confusing clarity. (Even the "solid" words the boys use are illusive: Piggy says "ass-mar" for asthma; Sam and Eric call themselves one name, "Sam 'n Eric.") Here is the first vision of the dead man in the tree:

> In front of them, only three or four yards away, was a rock-like hump where no rock should be. Ralph could hear a tiny chattering noise coming from somewhere—perhaps from his own mouth. He bound himself together with his will, fused his fear and loathing into a hatred, and stood up. He took two leaden steps forward.

> Behind them the sliver of moon had drawn clear of the horizon. Before them, something like a great ape was sitting asleep with its head between its knees. Then the wind roared in the forest, there was confusion in the darkness and the creature lifted its head, holding towards them the ruin of a face.

Golding gives us the short distance, the hulking object. Ralph (and the others) should be able to *see*. But he cannot. Although he "binds" himself—becoming more stable—he does not know where the noise comes from or what the "no-rock" is. His senses cannot rule the elements. He, like the lifted face, is a ruin.

V.S. Pritchett claims that *Lord of the Flies* indicates "Golding's desire to catch the sensation of things coming into us." On the contrary, it indicates his need to tell us that "out there" and "in here" never marry—not even on an enchanted island. We should not forget that the Lord of the Flies may be only a skull—an object given miraculous life because of faulty vision.

The Case for Strict Law and Order

Kathleen Woodward

Kathleen Woodward argues that *Lord of the Flies* presents a convincing case for democracy's strict enforcement of laws against violent behavior. Woodward uses *The Hunters*, a film about a primitive society, to clarify her argument. She shows that though Golding's primitive social group comprises essentially the same characters as the hunter society, it lacks conditions that bind individual members into a unified group capable of maintaining civil behavior. When Golding's schoolboys turn on one another with words and weapons, no authority or institutions stop them. Kathleen Woodward has researched myths, aging, and memory. She is the author of *At Last, The Real Distinguished Thing: The Late Poems of Eliot, Pound, Stevens, and Williams.*

Aptly described as an anthropological passion play [by Bernard F. Dick], *Lord of the Flies* is an inquiry into the politics of cohesion and conflict which attempts to show how the social bond disintegrates and eventually explodes into war. Golding's acute differentiation of the social roles of the four major characters invites comparison with the four-member hunting team of a primitive tribe as it is portrayed in John Marshall's classic ethnographic[1] film *The Hunters* and analyzed by the cultural historian William Irwin Thompson. According to this research, a successful hunting team in a tribal community requires four men, each of whom play different roles but all of whom work closely together. . . .

In Thompson we find a form of nostalgia for the harmonious interdependence and structural stability of the primi-

1. pertaining to the branch of anthropology that deals with the scientific development of specific human cultures

From "On Aggression: William Golding's *Lord of the Flies*" by Kathleen Woodward, in *No Place Else: Explorations in Utopian and Dystopian Fiction,* edited by Eric S. Rabkin, Martin H. Greenberg, and Joseph D. Olander. Copyright ©1983 by the Board of Trustees, Southern Illinois University. Reprinted by permission of Southern Illinois University Press.

tive community symbolized by the hunting team. He implies that politically it is superior because it encourages (indeed, demands) the development of individual talent in an atmosphere of cooperation, not competition. Extreme division of labor is not institutionalized, information is shared equally, and the members of the team respect each other's skills. The four perform in a sophisticated and highly coordinated way as a set of complementary opposites, as mapped below with the corresponding characters from *Lord of the Flies*:

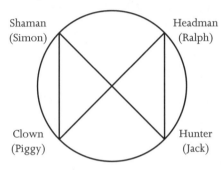

Shaman (Simon) — Headman (Ralph)

Clown (Piggy) — Hunter (Jack)

Left Side: Ideational[2]   Right Side: Operational

• Ralph is the *Headman*, the leader who is the person best suited for the position but also the equal of the others. Once given the authority, he shows genuine leadership, learning to assess his limitations and to seek good counsel. As the plot progresses, his sense of responsibility and reality—that is, disillusionment—grows.

• Piggy is the *Clown*, the most intelligent of the four and the voice of common sense.

• Simon is the *Shaman*, whose religious sensibility and insight into the dark interior of man's nature are essential to the community. It is Simon who grasps both the literal and metaphorical meaning of the beast—the Beast from the Sea is a dead man who is feared, as we must fear our own potential for violence—and who tries to impart this to the others.

• Jack is the *Hunter*, intent, obsessive, skillful, and possessed of stamina.

Whereas Thompson views his model of the primitive community as utopian, Golding's fiction of the anthropological primal scene is pessimistic. The origins of human society, he implies, are rooted in conflict, because human nature

2. pertaining to the imagination

is basically evil. The important point for us here is that while the spectrum of Golding's characterization corresponds to that portrayed in *The Hunters*, the *structuring* of their activity does not. What goes wrong? Must things break up? The problem is not that the psychological make-up of the four boys is deficient, that they each lack something essential. Rather, Golding's theory of the "essential illness" in human nature which existed from the beginning and which inevitably erupts in violence can be submitted to a structuralist critique. The point is that in *Lord of the Flies* the social bond did not exist from the start (nor is there any real reason for it to exist) and that Golding presents us with a completely unrealistic model of the origins of human politics. Furthermore, Golding does not so much show us how a state of peace under a rational form of government breaks down, as he shows us how the conceivably pleasant condition of anarchy disintegrates under the pressure of aggression.

GOLDING'S CHARACTERS FAIL ACCORDING TO THOMPSON'S MODEL

Thompson's model is completely inverted. On Golding's coral island, none of the four central characters is allowed to play his role properly. Unlike the situation in *The Hunters*, the four members of the elite in *Lord of the Flies* basically do not respect each other, do not share information appropriately, and do not divide labor in a beneficial way. Under these conditions, we should not be surprised that tension grows increasingly corrosive. While Piggy's essential role as the Clown is to make fun of the others, thus deflating their arrogance, they ridicule him instead, feeling superior to his ludicrously fat body and his school-marmish, no-nonsense attitude. Even Ralph, who comes to value Piggy's intelligence, feels that "Piggy was a bore; his fat, his ass-mar and his matter-of-fact ideas were dull, but," he admits to himself, "there was always a little pleasure to be got out of pulling his leg, even if one did it by accident." This is more destructive than simple dislike; on the part of the older boys, it is pure prejudice, for it is Piggy's physical nature—his debilitating asthma, his near blindness without his thick glasses, his pale fat body—which they despise. If Piggy is detested as an outsider, somebody who is "different," Simon is not esteemed for his mystical gifts. The role of the Shaman is to work magic when necessary, but Simon's vision into the meaning of things, which is quite accurate, is ignored. Worse, he is killed in the process of trying to reveal just what he does understand, and it is precisely his knowledge which would have delivered them from an unreasoning fear. He is misperceived as the Beast itself. Jack, the Hunter, hunts alone or only with his hunters (whom he completely dominates in a political hierarchy which he establishes) rather than with an interdisciplinary team, and thus inverts the process of hunting for the sake of survival to that of hunting to murder one of his own kind. And the Headman, Ralph, finds his leadership challenged from the very beginning. In addition, he makes several critical errors in judgment. He is wrong to delegate the responsibility for maintaining the fire to Jack and his hunters, and he is wrong to leave Piggy behind in the very beginning after the three of them decide to go off and explore the island. . . .

GOLDING'S SOCIETY LACKS KEY INGREDIENTS

If Golding's fable is brilliant in what it includes—his characterization is remarkably discerning—it is also ruthless in what it excludes. As a microcosm of the world at large, it self-consciously eliminates crucial aspects of society which create tension but, more importantly, provide purpose and generate binding social structures in the process.

First, Golding dismisses the basic problem of scarcity, which necessitates the organization of work. Fruit and fresh water are abundant, and the climate is tropical. The island is a leisure world where habits of discipline are superfluous. While the younger children play at the sea's edge, the older children play at being grown up. Voting and the right to free speech, the paraphernalia of democracy, are toys to them. The kids have only one urgent task—to keep the rescue fire going—and even this they are incapable of doing, for with few exceptions, their sense of the future gives way to instant gratification. Essentially they are playing a waiting game, and they invent dangerous games to pass the time.

Perhaps even more significant than Golding's bracketing of the problem of scarcity is his choice of a homogeneous group of middle-class white children, all of whom are boys, as a representative cross-section of society. There is no racial tension, no sexual tension, no tension of cultural difference. By populating his story with young boys only, all twelve and under, Golding removes the fundamental adhesive of society—the family. There are no kinship structures whatsoever, no bonds of love or even close friendship among these boys. It is tragically ironic that none of the boys are related by blood—and are eventually polarized by the desire to shed it. Thus the "society" which Golding portrays is *not* a society, but rather a collection of people. It has no objective (other than to prepare its own rescue, and not everyone agrees to that). It cannot even reproduce itself. It is small wonder that it turns pathological.[3]

But this was not Golding's purpose. He intended to show that violence in society arises out of man's very nature, his instincts. Firmly believing that violence is congenital,[4] "the terrible disease of being human" and not the result of faulty social organization, Golding makes no apologies for the parameters of his fiction. . . .

A WORLD IN MINIATURE

In this excerpt, Bernard F. Dick argues that Golding's exclusive use of children as characters in his novel limits exploration into the problem of evil.

Isolating the moral dichotomy in a group of boys invariably robs the work of any tragic stature it might possess. When children revert to bestiality, one can only say, "the horror, the horror." There is no catharsis because there is no poetry or tragic flaw; children are incapable of either. There is no real understanding of the evil that has erupted because children are too immature to associate cause with effect; Ralph may experience an undefined glimpse into "the darkness of man's heart" (and here again Golding is looking at Ralph as if he were an adult, giving him the tragic awareness of a hero); but, as a twelve-year-old, he cannot raise this new-found knowledge into a cosmic vision. Golding himself is not at fault here; given such a theme, one cannot imagine a better treatment. The island setting further simplifies the action, reducing it to a microcosm, or perhaps even a geocosm. The work is small-scaled in both setting and character, but it reproduces man and his world in miniature.

But what does Golding mean when he says violence arises "simply and solely out of the nature of the brute"? In

3. departure or deviation from a normal condition; sick   4. existing at or before birth; inherent

part, Golding has misread the moral of his own fiction. The moral of the story, he has said, is that "the shape of society must depend on the ethical nature of the individual and not on any political system." First, on the contrary, *Lord of the Flies* dramatizes, with power, how a society—like our own, not like a tribal community—can degenerate into lawlessness when there seems to be no apparent need to work with each other, no kinship ties binding people together, and no long-range social purpose but instead an emphasis on immediate satisfaction. Affluence, as we have seen, brings its own dangers. And secondly, it is more accurate, I think, to read *Lord of the Flies* as an argument for strict law and order within the democratic system rather than as a resigned plea that the shape of society depends on the upstanding ethical nature of a few individuals. . . .

The boys bring with them the knowledge of a democratic form of government, as they do a taste for violence. The conflict, which Golding so superbly articulates, is between the order of democratically arrived at rules and the expression of aggressive instincts. There is no question that to Golding's mind democracy is the preferred form of government. He presents it as humane and wise, as infinitely preferable to the insanities of an authoritarian regime. Piggy, the spectacle-wearing intellectual, puts it neatly, and there must be no hesitation on our part about the answer: "'Which is better—to have rules and agree, or to hunt and kill? . . . Which is better, law and rescue, or hunting and breaking things up?'" In Golding's fable, furthermore, the electorate, uninformed as it is, makes the best choice after all.

But what if Roger had been elected chief? Or Jack?

LORD OF THE FLIES ARGUES FOR STRICTER RULES

Golding's view of a democratic form of government is itself naive and innocent. It is clear to us that, unjust as it is, democracy in its "pure" form is not hardy enough to contain aggression. The moral to be drawn from the story is that the sweet persuasions of democracy must be sharpened by force. When Ralph asks Piggy midway through the narrative, "'What makes things break up like they do?'" Piggy's response is deadly accurate. "'I expect it's him,'" he answers, "'Jack.'" Although Golding suggests that everyone has the potential for letting blood—all of the children participate in the killing of Simon—Jack has a greater lust for it than the others. His regime is built on repression and violence. It cannot be combatted with the peaceful measures of democracy. Reason, indignation, and self-assertion, all of which Ralph try, will not work. Near the end of the story when Ralph goes up the mountain to demand Piggy's spectacles and to urge Jack and his band to help maintain the rescue fire, we know Ralph is being naive. He goes unarmed, underestimating the pathology of power.

Nor will the politics of isolation work. Piggy, Ralph, and the twins Sam and Eric try to hold down "civilization" and look after the little ones on the beach, but they are raided by Jack and his hunters, who have established a fort above them. The analogy to this is civil conflict or international war. One must fight back. Aggression requires aggression. But this Ralph never quite realizes. His form of government is constantly on the defensive, and thus he allows the situation to skid out of control. Ralph experiences a growth in moral consciousness—and this makes him sympathetic to us—but not a honing of his sense of *realpolitik*.[5] A curtain flaps sporadically in his brain, as his hold on reality goes dumb and he loses the power of speech.

The only way that the *force* of reason can prevail is to smash Jack's political machine, which involves us in an unpleasant contradiction that Golding does not face (England was forced to go to war against Hitler, and Golding would certainly agree that such action was required). Thus, on Golding's coral island, it is not that the shape of society must depend on the ethical nature of the individual but that the ethics of the democratic system must be bent in order to perpetuate that system. Institutions of discipline and punishment must be erected. In the course of the narrative Jack turns into a Charles Manson or an Idi Amin who should be hunted down as a public enemy, assassinated by a CIA, or incarcerated in a penal colony. At one point, during a meeting, Ralph shouts in exasperation to Jack, "'You're breaking the rules!'" Jack responds, "'Who cares?'" And Ralph can only answer, "'Because the rules are the only thing we've got!'" He's right, but the problem is that there are not *enough* rules: a system of rules is necessary for when the rules are broken.

Those rules come from the adult world, which is absent. Without them and the power to enforce them, incipient

5. practical politics having advancement of the national interest as its sole principle

democracy breaks down. Jack, the leader of the hunters, is the first to draw a knife to slice into animal flesh, but initially something holds him back—"the unbearable blood." This inhibition, this taboo, this remnant of custom, quickly fades. The second time around, Jack kills the pig with ease, with, in fact, triumphant abandon. "'You should have seen the blood!'" he exclaims. . . .

Ralph and Piggy, the two characters who steadfastly support democracy and refer to their upbringing in England positively, believe that the adult world provides appropriate models of behavior, and though they are partly naive about this too, they are basically right. Ralph's standard is "the memory of his sometime clean self." He invents a kind of fairy tale about adults *for* children, daydreaming of the cottage on the moor where he lived with his parents before he was sent away to school: there were wild ponies, cornflakes with cream and sugar, and good books to read. What sustained this "utopian" middle-class environment was discipline and English tradition, as well as love. "'Grownups know things,'" Piggy remarks elsewhere. "'They ain't afraid of the dark. They'd meet and have tea and discuss. Then things would be alright.'" It's possible. Realism and maturity might help one to see clearly, diplomacy might work. And we add, if they don't, institutions of punishment exist to repress undesirable behavior. It is in this sense that the political implications of *Lord of the Flies* are conservative, as they always are when someone believes that human nature is basically evil. Given the story, we are forced to conclude that law and order are the prime political issues and that it is better to impose and accept tradition than ever allow the rules to go slack.

CHAPTER 3

Techniques and Conventions in *Lord of the Flies*

READINGS ON
LORD OF THE FLIES

A Serious and Disquieting Story

E.M. Forster

E.M. Forster, who calls *Lord of the Flies* a serious book, says that even though William Golding has created an improbable situation, the characters resemble real people with believable human traits. As the boys revert to savagery, Forster argues that they become political and psychological symbols, and the novel becomes an investigation into the dark side of human nature present as well in the adults who rescue the boys at the end. British novelist E.M. Forster's work first appeared in 1905. His *A Passage to India* attracted attention for its insight into the British raj. Forster's writing has lent itself to cinematic interpretation, as three of his books, *A Room with a View*, *Howard's End*, and *A Passage to India* have become feature films. He also wrote short stories and essays and cowrote a libretto for the opera *Billy Budd.*

It is a pleasure and an honour to write [about *Lord of the Flies*], but there is also a difficulty, for the reason that the book contains surprises, and its reader ought to encounter them for himself. If he knows too much he will lean back complacently. And complacency is not a quality that Mr. Golding values. The universe, in his view, secretes something that we do not expect and shall probably dislike, and he here presents the universe, under the guise of a school adventure story on a coral island.

How romantically it starts! Several bunches of boys are being evacuated during a war. Their plane is shot down, but the "tube" in which they are packed is released, falls on an island, and having peppered them over the jungle slides into the sea. None of them are hurt, and presently they collect and prepare to have a high old time. A most improbable start. But Mr. Golding's magic is already at work and he persuades us to accept it. And though the situation is improbable the boys are not. He understands them thoroughly, partly through innate sympathy, partly because he has spent much of his life teaching. He makes us feel at once that we are with real human beings, even if they are small ones, and thus lays a solid foundation for the horrors to come.

Meet three boys.

THREE SYMBOLIC CHARACTERS

Ralph is aged a little over twelve. He is fair and well built, might grow into a boxer but never into a devil, for he is sunny and decent, sensible, considerate. He doesn't understand a lot, but has two things clear: firstly, they will soon be rescued—why, his daddy is in the Navy!—and secondly, until they are rescued they must hang together. It is he who finds the conch and arranges that when there is a meeting he who holds the conch shall speak. He is chosen as leader. He is democracy. And as long as the conch remains, there is some semblance of cooperation. But it gets smashed.

Meet Piggy.

Piggy is stout, asthmatic, shortsighted, underprivileged and wise. He is the brains of the party. It is the lenses of his spectacles that kindle fire. He also possesses the wisdom of the heart. He is loyal to Ralph, and tries to stop him from making mistakes, for he knows where mistakes may lead to in an unknown island. He knows that nothing is safe, nothing is neatly ticketed. He is the human spirit, aware that the universe has not been created for his convenience, and doing the best he can. And as long as he survives there is some semblance of intelligence. But he too gets smashed. He hurtles through the air under a rock dislodged by savages. His skull cracks and his brains spill out.

Meet Jack.

Jack is head of a choir—a bizarre assignment considering his destiny. He marches them two and two up the sun-drenched beach. He loves adventure, excitement, foraging in groups, orders when issued by himself, and though he does not yet know it and shrinks from it the first time, he loves shedding blood. Ralph he rather likes, and the liking is mutual. Piggy he despises and insults. He is dictatorship versus democracy. It is possible to read the book at a political level, and to see in its tragic trend the tragedy of our inter-war world. There is no doubt as to whose side the author is on here. He is on Ralph's. But if one shifts the vision to a still deeper level—the psychological—he is on the side of Piggy. Piggy knows that things mayn't go well because he knows what boys are, and he knows that the island, for all its apparent friendliness, is equivocal.

THE DISQUIETING OUTCOME

The hideous accidents that promote the reversion to savagery fill most of the book, and the reader must be left to endure them—and also to embrace them, for somehow or other they are entangled with beauty. The greatness of the vision transcends what is visible. At the close, when the boys are duly rescued by the trim British cruiser, we find ourselves on their side. We have shared their experience and resent the smug cheeriness of their rescuers. The naval officer is a bit disappointed with what he finds—everyone filthy dirty, swollen bellies, faces daubed with clay, two missing at least and the island afire. It ought to have been more like Coral Island, he suggests.

> Ralph looked at him dumbly. For a moment he had a fleeting picture of the strange glamour that had once invested the beaches. But the island was scorched up like dead wood— Simon was dead—and Jack had ... The tears began to flow and sobs shook him. He gave himself up to them now for the first time on the island; great, shuddering spasms of grief that seemed to wrench his whole body. His voice rose under the black smoke before the burning wreckage of the island; and infected by that emotion, the other little boys began to shake and sob too. And in the middle of them, with filthy body, matted hair, and unwiped nose, Ralph wept for the end of innocence, the darkness of man's heart, and the fall through the air of the true, wise friend called Piggy.

This passage—so pathetic—is also revealing. Phrases like "the end of innocence" and "the darkness of man's heart" show us the author's attitude more clearly than has appeared hitherto. He believes in the Fall of Man and perhaps in Original Sin. Or if he does not exactly believe, he fears; the same fear infects his second novel, a difficult and profound work called *The Inheritors*. Here the innocent (the boys as it were) are Neanderthal Man, and the corrupters are Homo Sapiens, our own ancestors, who eat other animals, discover intoxicants, and destroy. Similar notions occur in his other novels.

JACK'S DISRESPECT FOR PIGGY

After the boys mistakenly set the island on fire instead of sending up a small smoke signal, they meet on the mountain. This excerpt from chapter 2 illustrates Piggy's accurate and intelligent assessment of the situation and Jack's disregard and hatred for Piggy.

"You said you wanted a small fire and you been and built a pile like a hayrick. If I say anything," cried Piggy, with bitter realism, "you say shut up; but if Jack or Maurice or Simon— . . . You got your small fire all right."

Startled, Ralph realized that the boys were falling still and silent, feeling the beginnings of awe at the power set free below them. The knowledge and the awe made him savage.

"Oh, shut up!"

"I got the conch," said Piggy, in a hurt voice. "I got a right to speak."

They looked at him with eyes that lacked interest in what they saw, and cocked ears at the drum-roll of the fire. Piggy glanced nervously into hell and cradled the conch.

"We got to let that burn out now. And that was our fire-wood."

He licked his lips.

"There ain't nothing we can do. We ought to be more careful. I'm scared—"

Jack dragged his eyes away from the fire.

"You're always scared. Yah—Fatty!". . .

Piggy lost his temper.

"I got the conch! Just you listen! The first thing we ought to have made was shelters down there by the beach. It wasn't half cold down there in the night. But the first time Ralph says 'fire' you goes howling and screaming up this here mountain. Like a pack of kids!"

By now they were listening to the tirade.

"How can you expect to be rescued if you don't put first things first and act proper?"

Thus his attitude approaches the Christian: we are all born in sin, or will all lapse into it. But he does not complete the Christian attitude, for the reason that he never introduces the idea of a Redeemer. When a deity does appear, he is the Lord of the Flies, Beelzebub, and he sends a messenger to prepare his way before him.

The approach of doom is gradual. When the little boys land they are delighted to find that there are no grown-ups about. Ralph stands on his head with joy, and led by him they have a short period of happiness. Soon problems arise, work has to be assigned and executed, and Ralph now feels "we must make a good job of this, as grownups would, we mustn't let them down." Problems increase and become terrifying. In his desperation the child cries, "If only they could get a message to us, if only they could send us something grown-up . . . a sign or something." And they do. They send something grown-up. A dead parachutist floats down from the upper air, where they have been killing each other, is carried this way and that by the gentle winds, and hooks onto the top of the island.

This is not the end of the horrors. But it is the supreme irony. And it remains with us when the breezy rescuers arrive at the close and wonder why a better show wasn't put up.

Lord of the Flies is a very serious book which has to be introduced seriously. The danger of such an introduction is that it may suggest that the book is stodgy. It is not. It is written with taste and liveliness, the talk is natural, the descriptions of scenery enchanting. It is certainly not a comforting book. But it may help a few grown-ups to be less complacent and more compassionate, to support Ralph, respect Piggy, control Jack, and lighten a little the darkness of man's heart. At the present moment (if I may speak personally) it is respect for Piggy that seems needed most. I do not find it in our leaders.

Golding Portrays Young Boys Accurately

Ian McEwan

Recalling his first reading of *Lord of the Flies* when he was thirteen, Ian McEwan argues that Golding realistically captures the interests and behavior of young boys. McEwan compares his own boarding-school experiences with the behavior of the boys in Golding's novel. In particular, he cites his fantasy of life without grown-ups, his schoolmates' inability to function effectively as a group, and their mindless pack attacks on victims. Ian McEwan is a novelist and short story writer. He has published *First Love, Last Rites, In Between the Sheets, The Cement Garden,* and *The Comfort of Strangers.* He has also written motion picture and television screenplays.

I read *Lord of the Flies* at boarding school when I was thirteen in an edition specially strengthened, without irony or, probably, much success, against the quotidian[1] savagery of schoolboys. The mint new copies were distributed in class one summer's afternoon. The double thickness cardboard covers were bright gold, the colour, it came to seem, of desert island sands and the author's name. It was the kind of book that crackled when first opened, and the binding glue gave off something faintly faecal, the smell, it was soon established, of little boys gorging on tropical fruit and 'caught short' on the beach. The text was enticingly clear, at one with the limpid waters of the lagoon. The novel's reputation must have reached me for I already knew that this was a serious book, written by a grown-up for the careful attention of other grown-ups. At that time I was eager to be involved in the ways of real books. I started on the first page hungrily

1. everyday, commonplace

and read too quickly for I formed the impression of a boy with an enormous scar and a bird that could talk. I began again, more slowly this time, and was initiated, though I could not know it at the time, into the process whereby writers teach you how to read. Not all scars are on people; this one was in the fabric of the jungle. And the cry of a bird could be echoed by, and therefore resemble, the cry of a boy.

Two related discoveries gave me immediate pleasure. The first was that in this, an adult book, adults and all their grey, impenetrable concerns were not prominent. Here was the very stuff of my fantasy life and of my favourite childhood reading. For years I had daydreamed of grown-ups conveniently and painlessly dissolved (I didn't want them to suffer in any way) leaving me and a handful of competent friends to surmount dangers without ever being called into tea. I had read *Treasure Island* and *The Coral Island* of course, and I knew all about the less respectable end of the tradition, Enid Blyton's Adventure series in which four chums and a dog broke up international crime rings in their summer holidays. What was so attractively subversive and feasible about Golding was his apparent assumption that in a child-dominated world things went wrong in a most horrible and interesting way. For—and this was the second discovery—I *knew* these boys. I knew what they were capable of. I had seen us at it. As far as I was concerned, Golding's island was a thinly disguised boarding school.

GOLDING'S CHARACTERS RESEMBLE REAL SCHOOLBOYS

As a contemporary of Ralph, Piggy and Jack, I felt intimately acquainted with their problems, the most pressing of which—since I didn't want the boys rescued—seemed to be the difficulty of talking something through in a group to a useful resolution. I read the accounts of the meetings round the conch, the inevitable drift and confusion, with anguished recognition. At the age of twelve or thirteen it was just possible, given a little privacy and necessity, to develop a line of thought alone, to reach some kind of hazy conclusion. To do this with a group of friends was near impossible. We were at an age when we craved secret societies, codes, invented rituals and hierarchies; these all needed talking through before the fun could begin and countless elements conspired to subvert us: pure excitement, competitiveness, aggression, horseplay, power play, boasting, the need to find

DISORDER IN THE ASSEMBLY

A long assembly described in chapter 5 of Lord of the Flies *is halted many times by interruptions, disruptive behavior, name-calling, and sudden shifts away from the subject. Jack strikes the final blow to the meeting by confronting Ralph.*

The conch was snatched from his hands and Piggy's voice shrilled. . . .

"What are we? Humans? Or animals? Or savages? What's grownups going to think? Going off—hunting pigs—letting fires out—and now!"

A shadow fronted him tempestuously.

"You shut up, you fat slug!". . .

"Jack! Jack! You haven't got the conch! Let him speak."

Jack's face swam near him.

"And you shut up! Who are you, anyway? Sitting there telling people what to do. You can't hunt, you can't sing—"

"I'm chief. I was chosen."

"Why should choosing make any difference? Just giving orders that don't make any sense—"

"Piggy's got the conch."

"That's right—favor Piggy as you always do—"

"Jack!"

Jack's voice sounded in bitter mimicry.

"Jack! Jack!"

"The rules!" shouted Ralph, "you're breaking the rules!"

"Who cares?"

Ralph summoned his wits.

"Because the rules are the only thing we've got!"

But Jack was shouting against him.

"Bollocks to the rules! We're strong—we hunt! If there's a beast, we'll hunt it down! We'll close in and beat and beat and beat—!"

He gave a wild whoop and leapt down to the pale sand. At once the platform was full of noise and excitement, scramblings, screams and laughter. The assembly shredded away and became a discursive and random scatter from the palms to the water and away along the beach, beyond night-sight.

a joke at every turn, wild, associative thinking and everyone talking at once. We could not organize a thing among ourselves. One's own thoughts melted away. ('Ralph was puzzled by the shutter that flickered in his brain. There was something he wanted to say; then the shutter had come down.') Golding knew all about us. In *Lord of the Flies* I saw the messiness and insufficiencies of my little society spread out before me. For the first time in my life I was reading a book which did not depend on unlikeable characters or villains for a source of tension or evil. What I had known, without ever giving the matter much thought, from my crowded, dormitory existence, was confirmed and clarified; life could be unhappily divisive, even go fabulously wrong, without anyone having to be extravagantly nasty. No one was to blame—it was how it was when we were together.

I was uneasy when I came to the last chapters and read of the death of Piggy and the boys hunting Ralph down in a mindless pack. Only that year we had turned on two of our number in a vaguely similar way. A collective and unconscious decision was made, the victims were singled out and as their lives became more miserable by the day, so the exhilarating, righteous urge to punish grew in the rest of us. Neither of the boys was an obvious candidate for victimization, neither was ugly, stupid or weak. One combed his hair with a parting we found rather too precise. The other had an intimate, confiding manner and was sometimes over-generous with his sweets. Together we convinced ourselves the two of them were intolerable. Alone, none of us could have contemplated the daily humiliations, the little tortures we, the invincible, unknowing pack, inflicted on these two boys. Their parents had no choice but to take them away. When the uncomprehending father of the boy with the neat hair came in his car to collect his son, no one dared defy the group by going out at the last moment to say goodbye.

It did not take me many years to discover that schoolboys have no monopoly on unreason and cruelty and that they are not the only ones incapable of settling differences with calm discussion. This, of course, is Golding's whole point. The boys set fire to their island paradise while their elders and betters have all but destroyed the planet. When yet another assembly breaks down and the boys scatter across the beach, Ralph, Piggy and Simon are left behind and begin to catalogue with yearning the many competent ways the grown-ups would have managed things better. Golding interjects: 'The three boys stood in the darkness, striving unsuccessfully to convey the majesty of adult life.' At thirteen I too had sufficient faith in adult life to be immune to Golding's irony. *Lord of the Flies* thrilled me with all the power a fiction can have because I felt indicted by it. All my friends were implicated too. It made me feel ashamed in a rather luxurious way. The novel brought realism to my fantasy life (the glowing, liberated world without grown-ups) and years later, when I came to write a novel myself, I could not resist the momentum of my childhood fantasies nor the power of Golding's model, for I found myself wanting to describe a closed world of children removed from the constraints of authority. I had no doubt that my children too would suffer from, rather than exult in, their freedom. Without realizing it at the time, I named my main character after one of Golding's.

I cannot break completely from the memory of my first reading of *Lord of the Flies*. Whatever else it might be, and it is clearly many things, it remains for me a finely observed novel about schoolboys, the way they talk and fall out and turn into imitation aeroplanes mid-sentence. The din of the lower school common room at the Bishop Wordsworth School was not wasted on Golding. After all, the satanic authority of the Lord of the Flies himself is conveyed in words that Golding might have used in the classroom. 'The Lord of the Flies spoke in the voice of a schoolmaster. "This has gone quite far enough. My poor misguided child, do you think you know better than I do?"' At the age of thirteen I was not to know that Golding was interested in far more than observing schoolboys and was making exemplary use of a limited experience for enormously ambitious and successful ends. I felt that odd elation induced by artistically achieved pessimism; as far as I was concerned, the novel's blaming finger was pointed at schoolboys like Jack, Piggy, Ralph and me. We were manifestly inadequate. We couldn't think straight, and in sufficiently large groups we were capable of atrocities. In that I took it all so personally, I like to think that I was, in some sense, an ideal reader.

Significant Motifs in *Lord of the Flies*

E.L. Epstein

E.L. Epstein argues that in *Lord of the Flies* William Golding addresses the central concern of major modern thinkers and scholars—the nature of the human personality. Epstein analyzes three of the novel's motifs: the pig's head as Beelzebub; the killing of the sow; and Simon's conversation with the Lord of the Flies. According to Epstein, these motifs portray the connection between the darkness within human nature and its connection to outer reality. E.L. Epstein has taught at Queens College of the City University of New York. He is the author of *Language and Style* and *The Ordeal of Stephen Dedalus: Conflict of the Generations in James Joyce's* A Portrait of the Artist as a Young Man.

The theme of *Lord of the Flies* is described by Golding as follows . . . : "The theme is an attempt to trace the defects of society back to the defects of human nature. The moral is that the shape of a society must depend on the ethical nature of the individual and not on any political system however apparently logical or respectable. The whole book is symbolic in nature except the rescue in the end where adult life appears, dignified and capable, but in reality enmeshed in the same evil as the symbolic life of the children on the island. The officer, having interrupted a man-hunt, prepares to take the children off the island in a cruiser which will presently be hunting its enemy in the same implacable way. And who will rescue the adult and his cruiser?"

This is, of course, merely a casual summing-up on Mr. Golding's part of his extremely complex and beautifully woven symbolic web which becomes apparent as we follow through the book, but it does indicate that *Lord of the Flies* is not, to say the least, a simple adventure story of boys on a desert island. In fact, the implications of the story go far beyond the degeneration of a few children. What is unique about the work of Golding is the way he has combined and synthesized all of the characteristically twentieth-century methods of analysis of the human being and human society and used this unified knowledge to comment on a "test situation." In this book, as in few others at the present time, are findings of psychoanalysts of all schools, anthropologists, social psychologists and philosophical historians mobilized into an attack upon the central problem of modern thought: the nature of the human personality and the reflection of personality on society.

THE CENTRAL SYMBOL

Another feature of Golding's work is the superb use of symbolism, a symbolism that "works." The central symbol itself, the "lord of the flies," is, like any true symbol, much more than the sum of its parts; but some elements of it may be isolated. The "lord of the flies" is a translation of the Hebrew *Ba'alzevuv* (*Beelzebub* in Greek). It has been suggested that it was a mistranslation of a mistransliterated[1] word which gave us this pungent and suggestive name for the Devil, a devil whose name suggests that he is devoted to decay, destruction, demoralization, hysteria and panic and who therefore fits in very well with Golding's theme.

The Devil is not present in any traditional religious sense; Golding's Beelzebub is the modern equivalent, the anarchic, amoral, driving force that Freudians call the Id, whose only function seems to be to insure the survival of the host in which it is embedded or embodied, which function it performs with tremendous and single-minded tenacity. Although it is possible to find other names for this force, the modern picture of the personality, whether drawn by theologians or psychoanalysts, inevitably includes this force or psychic structure as the fundamental principle of the Natural Man. The tenets of civilization, the moral and social codes, the Ego, the intelligence itself, form only a veneer over this white-hot power, this uncontrollable force, "the fury and the mire of human veins.". . . One could, if one were

---

1. an error made in the process of representing a word in the corresponding characters of another alphabet

so minded, go through the entire canon of modern literature, philosophy and psychology and find this great basic
drive defined as underlying the most fundamental conclusions of modern thought.

THE CENTRAL SYMBOL LEADS TO THEME

The emergence of this concealed, basic wildness is the
theme of the book; the struggle between Ralph, the representative of civilization with his parliaments and his brain
trust (Piggy, the intellectual whose shattering spectacles
mark the progressive decay of rational influence as the story
progresses), and Jack, in whom the spark of wildness burns
hotter and closer to the surface than in Ralph and who is the
leader of the forces of anarchy on the island, is also, of
course, the struggle in modern society between those same
forces translated onto a worldwide scale.

THE SYMBOLIC KILLING OF THE SOW

The turning point in the struggle between Ralph and Jack is
the killing of the sow. The sow is a mother: "sunk in deep
maternal bliss lay the largest of the lot . . . the great bladder
of her belly was fringed with a row of piglets that slept or
burrowed and squeaked." The killing of the sow is accom-
plished in terms of sexual intercourse.

> They were just behind her when she staggered into an open
> space where bright flowers grew and butterflies danced
> round each other and the air was hot and still.
>
> Here, struck down by the heat, the sow fell and the hunters
> hurled themselves at her. This dreadful eruption from an un-
> known world made her frantic; she squealed and bucked and
> the air was full of sweat and noise and blood and terror.
> Roger ran round the heap, prodding with his spear whenever
> pigflesh appeared. Jack was on top of the sow, stabbing
> downward with his knife. Roger [a natural sadist, who be-
> comes the "official" torturer and executioner for the tribe]
> found a lodgment for his point and began to push till he was
> leaning with his whole weight. The spear moved forward
> inch by inch, and the terrified squealing became a high-
> pitched scream. Then Jack found the throat and the hot blood
> spouted over his hands. The sow collapsed under them and
> they were heavy and fulfilled upon her. The butterflies still
> danced, preoccupied in the center of the clearing.

The pig's head is cut off; a stick is sharpened at both ends
and "jammed in a crack" in the earth. (The death planned
for Ralph at the end of the book involves a stick sharpened

at both ends.) The pig's head is impaled on the stick; ". . . the head hung there, a little blood dribbling down the stick. Instinctively the boys drew back too; and the forest was very still. They listened, and the loudest noise was the buzzing of flies over the spilled guts." Jack offers this grotesque trophy to "the Beast," the terrible animal that the littler children had been dreaming of, and which seems to be lurking on the island wherever they were not looking. The entire incident forms a horrid parody of an Oedipal[2] wedding night; these emotions, the sensations aroused by murder and death, and the overpowering and unaccustomed emotions of sexual love experienced by the half-grown boys, plus their own irrational fears and blind terrors, release the forces of death and the devil on the island.

SIMON'S INTERVIEW WITH THE HEAD

After this occurs the most deeply symbolic incident in the book, the "interview" of Simon, an embryo mystic, with the head. The head seems to be saying, to Simon's heightened perceptions, that "everything was a bad business. . . . The half-shut eyes were dim with the infinite cynicism of adult life." Simon fights with all his feeble power against the message of the head, against the "ancient, inescapable recognition," the recognition of human capacities for evil and the superficial nature of human moral systems. It is the knowledge of the end of innocence, for which Ralph is to weep at the close of the book. "'Fancy thinking the Beast was something you could hunt and kill!' said the head. For a moment or two the forest and all the other dimly appreciated places echoed with the parody of laughter. 'You knew, didn't you? I'm part of you? Close, close, close! I'm the reason why it's no go? Why things are what they are?'"

At the end of this fantastic scene Simon imagines he is looking into a vast mouth. "There was blackness within, a blackness that spread. . . . Simon was inside the mouth. He fell down and lost consciousness." This mouth, the symbol of ravenous, unreasoning and eternally insatiable nature, appears again in *Pincher Martin,*[3] in which the development of the theme of a Nature inimical to the conscious personality of man is developed in a stunning fashion. In *Lord of the*

2. relating to the Oedipus complex, a subconscious sexual desire in a child, especially a male child, for the parent of the opposite sex   3. by William Golding

Flies, however, only the outline of a philosophy is sketched, and the boys of the island are figures in a parable or fable which like all great parables or fables reveals to the reader an intimate, disquieting connection between the innocent, time-passing, story-telling aspect of its surface and the great, "dimly appreciated" depths of its interior.

Golding's Deliberately Obscure Setting

Bernard S. Oldsey and Stanley Weintraub

Bernard S. Oldsey and Stanley Weintraub argue that Golding has made the setting of *Lord of the Flies*—its time and place—intentionally vague. The story unfolds in some unreal present-future time, and, lacking geography, takes place on an island in the Indian or Pacific Ocean. The authors have imagined a map of the island on which they identify the sites of major events. The vagueness of the setting, Oldsey and Weintraub argue, gives the work qualities of both a realistic novel and an allegorical fable. Bernard S. Oldsey and Stanley Weintraub have taught English at Pennsylvania State University. Weintraub is the author of *The Yellow Book: Quintessence of the Nineties* and *Reggie: A Portrait of Reginald Turner.* Oldsey is the coauthor of *Visions and Revisions in Modern American Literary Criticism* and *From Fact to Judgment.*

Lord of the Flies (1954), Golding's first novel and the one that established his reputation, is still most widely acclaimed as his major work. Not only has it captured a large segment of the popular and academic imagination (having the effect there of replacing J.D. Salinger's *The Catcher in the Rye*), but it has also attracted the greatest amount of critical attention directed toward Golding. . . .

Golding is essentially a literary man who uses scene, character, and symbol (not to mention an exceedingly fine style and some admittedly tricky plot methods) to achieve imaginative literary effects.

The scenic qualities of *Lord of the Flies* help make it an imaginative work for the reader as well as the author. Although Golding occasionally provides consolidating detail,

Excerpts from *The Art of William Golding* by Bernard S. Oldsey and Stanley Weintraub. Copyright ©1965 and renewed 1993 by Bernard S. Oldsey and Stanley Weintraub. Reprinted by permission of Harcourt Brace & Company.

he more commonly requires the reader to pull narrative and descriptive elements into focus. For example, he provides no end-paper map or block description of his fictional island. The reader must explore it along with the participants in the story and piece together a usable concept of time and place. What we learn in this way is just enough to keep the work within the realm of fiction, but not enough to remove it from the realm of allegory. *And the essence of Golding's art resides exactly within the area of overlap.*

Fable-like, time and place are vague. The Queen (Elizabeth?) still reigns, and "Reds" are apparently the vague enemy. It is the postcatastrophic near-future, in which nuclear war has laid waste much of the West. ("They're all dead," Piggy thinks. And "civilization," corroborates Golding, is "in ruins.") The fiery crash of the boys' plane upon a tropical island has been the final stage of their evacuation from England. The island seems to lie somewhere in the Indian or Pacific Ocean, probably on a line extending from England to Australia, which could well have been the planned terminus of their evacuation. Jack provides the clue for such geographical extrapolation when he speaks of Simon's seizures at "Gib." (Gibraltar) and "Addis" (Addis Ababa[1]), as well as "at matins over the pre-centor."[2]

THE ISLAND SETTING

Shaped roughly like an outrigged boat, the boys' haven is a tropical island with a coral base. A mile out along one side runs a barrier reef, between which and the island lies a lagoon, on whose inward shore the boys hold their assemblies. At one end of the island there appears to be another, smaller island; but upon close inspection this is found to be attached by a rocky isthmus. Topographically, the island rises from low jungle and orchard land to a mountaintop, or ridge, with few or no trees. By way of food, it provides the boys with bananas, coconuts, an "olive-grey, jelly-like fruit," and wild pig, as well as crab and fish taken from the sea. At midday the island gets hot enough to produce mirage effects.

If there were an end-paper map for Golding's island, it would no doubt be marked to indicate these major points of interest: (1) the beach along the lagoon, where Piggy and

---

1. the capital and largest city of Ethiopia in the center of the country   2. the director of the choral services of a cathedral

SCENERY DESCRIBED IN COLOR AND IMAGES

Golding describes minor scenes and island detail in vivid colors, in sound images, and in images drawn from the animal world. Excerpts from chapter 2, when the boys explore the island, illustrate Golding's technique.

"Heave!"

The great rock loitered, posed on one toe, decided not to return, moved through the air, fell, struck, turned over, leapt droning through the air and smashed a deep hole in the canopy of the forest. Echoes and birds flew, white and pink dust floated, the forest further down shook as with the passage of an enraged monster: and then the island was still. . . .

It was roughly boat-shaped: humped near this end with behind them the jumbled descent to the shore. On either side rocks, cliffs, treetops and a steep slope: forward there, the length of the boat, a tamer descent, tree-clad, with hints of pink: and then the jungly flat of the island, dense green, but drawn at the end to a pink tail. There, where the island petered out in water, was another island; a rock, almost detached, standing like a fort, facing them across the green with one bold, pink bastion. . . .

The reef enclosed more than one side of the island, lying perhaps a mile out and parallel to what they now thought of as their beach. The coral was scribbled in the sea as though a giant had bent down to reproduce the shape of the island in a flowing chalk line but tired before he had finished. Inside was peacock water, rocks and weed showing as in an aquarium; outside was the dark blue of the sea. The tide was running so that long streaks of foam tailed away from the reef. . . .

Every point of the mountain held up trees—flowers and trees. Now the forest stirred, roared, flailed. The nearer acres of rock flowers fluttered and for half a minute the breeze blew cool on their faces. . . .

The bushes were dark evergreen and aromatic and the many buds were waxen green and folded up against the light. Jack slashed at one with his knife and the scent spilled over them.

Ralph find the conch, and where assemblies are held near a natural platform of fallen trees; (2) the mountaintop, from which the island is surveyed, where the signal fire is placed, and where eventually the dead parachutist is trapped by wind and rock; (3) the burned-out quarter mile, where the mulberry-faced boy dies in the first fire; (4) Simon's leafy bower, to which he makes mystic retreats and from which he views the ceremony of impaling the pig's head upon a stake; (5) the orchard, where the fruit is picked and where some of the "littluns" are "taken short," leaving behind their fecal trail; (6) the "castle" at the tail end of the island, rising a hundred feet from the sea, where the first search for the "beast" is made, and where Piggy is killed after Jack has made this bastion his headquarters; and (7) the jungle, with its hanging vines that recall snakes and "beasties," with its pig trails where Jack hunts and where Ralph is finally hunted.

When the details are extracted and given order under an analytical light, Golding's island looks naturalistic in specification. But matters are not at all that clear in the book. The location of the island, for example, is kept deliberately vague: it is sufficiently remote to draw only two ships in a month or so, yet close enough to "civilization" to be the floor above which deadly, and old-fashioned, air battles are fought miles high (the boys' plane itself has been shot down). The nearby air and naval war in progress, with conventional weapons, is somewhat out of keeping with earlier reports of utter catastrophe. Equally incongruous is the smartly attired naval officer and savior of the closing pages, whose jaunty mien is incompatible with catastrophe. Yet he is as important to the machinery of the allegory as the earlier crash, which is equally difficult to explain on rational grounds. During the crash the fuselage of the evacuation plane has apparently broken in two: the forward half (holding pilot and others, including more boys) has been cleanly washed out to sea by a conveniently concomitant storm; and the after-section (which makes a long fiery scar as it cuts through the jungle) tumbles unscathed children onto the island. As incompatible, obscure, askew, and unrealistic as these elements may be, they are no more so than Gulliver's adventures. And Golding's graphically novelistic character and topographic details, both poetic and naturalistic, tend to blur the fabulous qualities of the narrative's use of time and setting in its opening and close. Although it is enough to say that the fabulist must be permitted pegs upon which to hang his fable, it is Golding's richly novelistic elements of the telling that call attention to the subtle dissonance. Paradoxically—yet artistically—this very tension between realistic novel and allegorical fable imparts to *Lord of the Flies* some of its unique power.

Irony in *Lord of the Flies*

Henri Talon

Henri Talon argues that irony pervades *Lord of the Flies*. Readers find cruelty when they expect to find play. Characters' actions based on good principles produce deplorable results. Innocent choir boys reveal an inherent dark side, and at the end, the fire meant to destroy Ralph becomes the signal that brings a boat to rescue them. While irony usually sharpens understanding, which in turn leads to inspiration, the irony in this novel produces no hopeful or inspired outcome. Henri Talon has taught at the University of Dijon in France.

Lord of the Flies is a web of ironies. The very nature of this fable is ironic since it reveals cruelty and perversity where one expects to find gentleness and innocence—in childhood. Moreover, the children's sole intention at the start is to play: 'Until the grown-ups come to fetch us, we'll have fun,' says Ralph and, to begin with, he stands on his head. Can one imagine anything more harmless than the freedom from care, the roguishness and the joy of these new Crusoes? And yet, playing will prove to be a source of evil for them. It will bring about their regress and disaster. Thus irony—an essential discord in the story—is the form assumed here by the author's creative urge. . . .

PLAY DIFFERS FOR RALPH, PIGGY, AND JACK

How well one can understand Ralph's enthusiastic exclamations and capers! Playing opens a parenthesis in daily life; it is an escape from the adult world: 'Until the grown-ups come to fetch us, we'll have fun'. But next to Ralph is Piggy for whom playing is absurd. He declines to enter an imaginary universe which appears as the negation of common sense, thought, responsibility and worry. His asthma, myopia and lack of physical energy have never allowed him to

Excerpted from Henri Talon, "Irony in *Lord of the Flies*," *Essays in Criticism*, vol. 18, no. 3, July 1968. Reprinted by permission.

think that it would be good to conjure up a fantastic country in his auntie's very cottage and a dream interlude in the midst of homework.

The meaning of play as an interruption of the normal course of existence, as disregard and oblivion of time, is so foreign to him that he once suggested to the other boys, astonished and mocking, that they should make a sundial.

The moment Ralph gets the conch out of the water, Piggy proposes to establish a society inspired by that of the grown-ups. 'We can use this to call the others. Have a meeting. They'll come, when they hear us'. And when this proposal is enriched by Roger's hint that they ought to have a vote, Ralph is provided with just those factors of seriousness which make a game truly funny. A good game demands discipline. The harder the trial the greater the fun. . . .

But, very soon, acted seriousness, seriousness for fun, if I may bring together words that seem to clash, becomes real earnestness. The game is a game no longer. The role of chief [that] Ralph has assumed involves obligations that exclude pretence. The existence of time cannot be ignored or denied after all. Like Piggy, Ralph is torn between regret for the past and the hope of a doubtful return home, while Jack and his tribe are engrossed by the hunt and the dance and the swim which make their lives a continuous present.

Against all expectations, playing proves to be a school for Ralph, since it conduces to a keener sense of duty instead of blurring it; since it makes him realise his limitations instead of giving a glorious feeling of freedom and power. This is one of irony's many faces.

As for Jack, playing the part of chief of the hunters gratifies his love of physical effort and leadership, and his impatience with all but his own rules. However, for him also the game soon ceases to be mere play, a temporary forgetting of the serious business of life. Certainly playing ever involves seriousness too, as I have already remarked, yet the player is always aware that the importance of the game is of his own making and therefore different from the seriousness that life enforces upon us. But the seriousness of the game becomes the only one that Jack wishes to, and eventually can, recognize. His passion for hunting blinds him to other issues. The borderline between the *Spielwelt*[1] and the world outside,

1. playworld

never a very clear one to him, is being gradually erased. He is carried away by the love of violence and the bloodlust that killing pigs has aroused in him. And once he has smeared his face with war paint he yields to the demoniac power of the mask. . . .

[Golding] has found for himself a well-known psychological truth that serves his end in his fable—namely, that playing may give birth to obscure forces which overwhelm reason. And thus, when fear of the unknown and dread of the oncoming storm have brought the frenzy of the dance to its highest pitch, the children, half believing that Simon is the Beast in disguise, murder him. . . .

GOOD INTENTIONS TURN BAD

But let us carry further the analysis of a story in which human beings finally do harm although they first meant to do good, in which gestures falsify intentions and action appears as a caricature of design.

The children decide to build a society whose foundations will be freedom and justice. Whoever wishes to speak may do so, provided he respects the ritual and holds the conch, and everyone has a right to vote. Rules set down by unanimous consent should have been obeyed unreservedly. The discipline which Piggy and Ralph imagine is voluntary submission, the highest form of liberty, that which sets bounds to its own expression.

Such is the original purpose and option, but what happens? The right to speak leads to idle talk. 'We have lots of assemblies,' says Ralph, 'Everybody enjoys speaking and being together. We decide things. But then they don't get done'. They agree to build shelters and then go bathing instead of working. They agree to keep up a fire on the mountain top and forget it. They agree to observe elementary hygiene and to use as a lavatory rocks which the tide cleans up; but they soon use anywhere, even—supreme derision!—near the platform where they hold their meetings. They planned order and allowed disorder to settle. The hopes that initiate action are baffled by it in the end. The human being appears as an invalid whose rebellious hand plays his spirit false when the spirit is not first unfaithful to itself.

All this makes clear the nature of the irony that runs through the whole work. It is made manifest by contrast and conflict and is characterized by ambiguity, for the children's failure is nonetheless funny, but the fun is no true joy. The association of merriment and sadness is naturally paradoxical,[2] but irony flourishes in paradox—it calls up a smile and turns it into a grimace.

Why is this so? The reason is because we are divided against ourselves in the presence of irony. We readily perceive the comic in a social and political organisation which is but an apish simulacrum.[3] Yet we also detect in those brats' negligence and confusion a scaled-down version of adult disorder. Undecisive meetings, barren debates, misapplied or unenforced resolutions, we have experienced all this, and we feel the sadness of it all.

It is sad because disorder is prejudicial to everybody, and because it should never have been. The principles are good, the conduct they inspire deplorable. The beginning is full of promise, the end is a catastrophe. Between what is and what ought to have been there is a great gulf, and the cause is to be found in the very nature of man who is fated to fail for he is 'sick', as Simon puts it; and the heroism which this intuitive little boy also perceives is of no avail. Therefore, the irony of man's destiny is potentially in his own being. Here are perceptible the philosophical overtones of irony. Irony often appears when a man looks at himself, inquires into his sickness and attempts to probe his own mystery. Anyhow, the fabulist is ever urging us to pass from the observation of conduct to a reflection on being, from the collapse of society to the evil in man.

IRONIC CONNECTIONS BETWEEN THE BEGINNING AND THE END

Having shown the general orientation and scope of irony, we must further examine the structure of the narrative, since irony breaks out between contrasted scenes somewhat distant from one another, and even as far apart as the beginning and the end of the story.

For instance, when we first catch sight of Ralph, he is neat, handsome and laughing. He prepares to live an adventure that seems to have leapt into existence from one of his books. When we last see him he is dirty, in rags and sobbing. He had looked forward to a fine, clean game and he has lived a sordid, terrible drama. He had anticipated an episode

---

2. seeming to be contradictory   3. a foolish imitation or representation

as good as a dream and he has been through a nightmare. But in the interval the little boy has matured and he knows 'the darkness of man's heart'. The tears he sheds do not spring from self-pity. He weeps for Simon and Piggy who have died and for them all who have sinned. . . .

Jack also provides an instance of the irony that is discharged when scenes loaded with opposite meanings and as it were with different electricities clash in our memory—'After all,' he says soon after he has joined Ralph and Piggy, 'we're not savages. We're English; and the English are best at everything'. At each stage of his regress we remember his proud words. When, having bedaubed his face with paint, he looks at the image reflected in a coconut shell filled with water, it is not himself he sees but 'an awesome stranger'. The incident underscores the mistake he made in denying his kinship with savages, for, *in potentia*,[4] he was a savage even at the beginning. Didn't he leave the cloaked choirboys standing so long in the sun that Simon fainted away? The stranger whom the mirror has revealed to him is not an outsider. He has risen from the depths of his own nature.

In parts, the irony comes of the self-ignorance of a boy who thought that he was a law-abiding, righteous human being whereas, beneath the black coat adorned with a long silver cross, there was an uncivilized brute. The image of the togged-up choirboy contrasts with that of the undressed hunter ever brandishing his knife. Naked man, 'unaccommodated man' is no poor forked animal but a blood-thirsty brute. . . .

Jack did not try to deceive anyone. He believed in his own inborn virtue as an Englishman. . . . The naval officer's words at the end echo those which the boy utters at the beginning: 'I should have thought that a pack of British boys—you're all British aren't you?—would have been able to put up a better show than that.' Here irony spreads out like a fan.

It was impossible for the officer to guess what happened on the island. This is not a question of either self-deception or lack of imagination, as is often asserted by readers. This is the normal ignorance of one who never had any opportunity of observing the lawlessness to which small boys can yield when they are left to themselves for long. He sees dirty boys in rags, but precisely such slovenliness is what one ex-

4. potentially

pects from children. Everybody knows that children do not like to wash, perhaps because they are convinced, as was Anatole France's Petit Pierre,[5] that washing is useless since they are asked to do it again and again.

For the reader, the irony results from the contrast between the picture of puerile innocence which the officer thinks he is beholding, and our memory of their insane cruelty. It is untrue to say that the officer reminds us of what we had forgotten—that these devils were only children. No, the irony comes of the contradiction between the data of vision on the one hand, and those of memory on the other; it comes of the clash between what seems likely to the officer—namely that schoolboys have availed themselves of an extra vacation to indulge in pranks and games usually forbidden—a pleasant likelihood which is false—and the children's perversity which has been revealed to us—a terrible unlikelihood which is the truth.

The next ironic effect is due to the fact that the boys' rescue is no salvation, since they leave an island scorched up like dead wood to return to a world that is in the process of being burned down too. . . . The naval officer does not know either whether Ralph, whom he has snatched from the jaws of death today, will not be killed tomorrow. The boy leaves a demented society to join another, whose folly is not a whit less cruel. And can precociously corrupted children regain balance and normality among men equally perverted and abnormal?

THE BITTEREST IRONY OF ALL

There is to be found in this story a form of irony which is even more bitter, which no longer raises a smile, however wry, because the discord of which we are made aware rends both our heart and intellect. It is related to Simon's fate, the child who stands for *Agapé*,[6] whose courage springs from love, whose insight into man's heart is charismatic, and whose loneliness is great, precisely because he is exceptional.

When he is bold enough to say that they should seek the Beast in themselves—'What I mean is . . . maybe it's only us'—he causes indignation and laughter. They say he is 'cracked', he is 'batty'. They might have listened to a fluent, handsome, athletic boy, for they are as sensitive to physical

5. French novelist's character Little Pierre   6. spiritual love

strength and charm as indifferent to moral virtue and beauty. Simon cannot be understood, for he speaks the language of truth to the blind, that of humility to the proud. And when he endeavours to save his friends from their own passion by telling them that the Beast is harmless, he is assaulted not only by the wicked, but also by the righteous—the temporarily bewildered Ralph and Piggy—and he dies.

Here irony calls forth at once compassion for the victim and terror of the murderers, as it also does a two-fold moral judgment: respect for Simon, contempt of Jack and Roger. Indeed, the resonance of irony goes even deeper, for Ralph and Piggy are spared our scorn, although they are guilty. Our pity suspends condemnation.

THE IRONY OF WHO YOU ARE AND WHAT YOU DO

Again, we can observe that irony is associated with both doing and being. The contingent cause of Simon's murder lies in his misconception of the boys' state of mind and of the temper in the tribe, but he was predestined to such mistakes by his very selflessness. He is a victim because he is what he is. Irony is also related to the moral solitude of the innocent person among sinners. Nobody understands Simon, Piggy least of all, for whereas Simon is prompted by moral vision, Piggy only believes what can be explained and demonstrated—'Life's scientific'.

But Piggy is very lonely too, although he soon wins Ralph's pity and later deserves his regard. He is despised for he is not fit to play games. Should he make no mistakes he would nonetheless be spurned by the other boys; for being different amounts to a kind of culpability in their sight. Moreover, his very loneliness occasions his blunders. As he desperately needs sympathy, he rashly confides in Ralph, whose amiable unconcern towards him he mistakes for fellow-feeling. When Ralph's face brightens up because he is dreaming a happy dream, he interprets the light in the dreamer's eyes as the dawn of friendship, and responds by a cheerful laugh to a smile that was not meant for him.

Piggy makes mistakes because he is too unlike the others and left too much on his own to understand them. He lacks the experience that intelligence needs to operate successfully. His reasoning is often vitiated because his premises are wrong. When he makes up his mind to challenge Jack about his spectacles, it is obvious that he does not have an inkling of the other boy's motivation. His words are at once touching because they reveal how exacting his sense of justice is, and ridiculous, because they are unrealistic. 'I'm going to him with this conch in my hands,' he says, 'I don't ask for my glasses back . . . as a favour . . . but because what's right's right'.

This is an instance of the conflict between the *Eiron* and the *Alazon* which, in various forms, is a recurrent theme in comedy as in tragedy: *Eiron* being used here not in its original denotation—'a dissembler', but in its derivative meaning—'a naive' or even 'foolish' person. The honest, guileless one, backed up by Ralph, stands against the 'Impostor', whom we see on one occasion, sitting on his throne like an idol. The 'Impostor' wins the day, irony arises, and once again we are divided against ourselves. We grieve because justice is flouted and trampled down, but we cannot help smiling because Piggy is as short-sighted intellectually as physically. We are moved because his faith in democracy is admirable, but we are amused because he proclaims it when democracy is no longer.

IRONY USUALLY AWAKENS AND PAVES WAY FOR NEW ASPIRATIONS

Piggy stands for intelligence made inoperative because he is unaware of its limitations and starved by his ignorance of usual human intercourse. To a large extent his life is one of misunderstanding, and not only his. In this fictional universe, misunderstanding is general. . . .

Piggy's intelligence, valuable in spite of its shortcomings, is not recognized, neither is Simon's vision, which could have redeemed them, nor Ralph's good will and common sense, which should have enabled them to survive. The dead parachutist, a victim of man's folly, is not recognized for the poor, harmless thing he has become. Instead of uniting them in a common pity, he intensifies the irrational fear which brings about hatred and division.

Indeed the ironist is a stern Prosecutor. He condemns both Piggy who only believes in what is reasonable and Simon who fails to realise its necessity. He indicts Ralph who thinks that it is enough for a community to ensure the practical welfare of all. The rationalist, the visionary, the eudemonist[7]

7. the one who wishes to produce happiness

are all guilty because they all are mistaken. Golding's fable calls to mind the destructive character of irony considered strictly in itself. . . . Within the framework of the story it is hard to see on what values the author would lay a faith in the future of the human city.

Irony scours surfaces tarnished by routine use, it opens a man's eyes, it raises questions, but it answers none. It is, or should be, a turning point in the development of critical thinking before one comes to a new affirmation. Because it makes one's vision keener and more delicate it is an important state in the life of the Spirit, but it cannot gratify the very needs it contributes to awaken. . . .

Indeed the time comes all too quickly when Ralph becomes ironically aware of the contrast between his early hopes and happiness and the wearisomeness that followed. 'Remembering that first enthusiastic exploration as though it were part of a brighter childhood, he smiled jeeringly'. Thus irony operates first and foremost at the cost of the ironist. Ralph does not spare himself. Because he has matured, he finds the little chap he was not long ago at once touching and laughable. Now he knows what it means to age: he can look back and survey his short life; he has a history.

Later, when he and Jack have grown bitter enemies, he hesitates to summon an assembly for fear Jack and his tribe will not come. He feels that the breach will be irreparable the moment his authority is openly flouted. If he does not know whether or not to blow the conch, the reason is because, ironically, cowardice and courage look alike all of a sudden. Is it dastardly to refuse to acknowledge the secession that has taken place, or is it moral strength, the strength of a ruler who temporizes as long as there is a hope for the better? 'If I blow the conch and they don't come back, then we've had it. We shan't keep the fire going. We'll be like animals. We'll never be rescued'.

Ralph also experiences the grim derision that lies in that last effort of his to bring the boys together, when only 'the littluns'—a useless audience—turn up. And when Piggy says to him: 'You're still Chief,' the loyalty of his one friend gives a sharper edge to his loneliness, for nothing remains of the former order except the now unavailing conch and that vain, inept title in which Piggy still believes.

He laughs sharply, and Piggy is frightened. This is the laughter of that brand of irony which is sometimes called romantic, that of lost illusions; an irony that may be light and gentle but that sometimes expresses despair. If Piggy asks Ralph to stop laughing, it is because he feels that his friend is on the brink of tears.

However, Ralph's spiritual development does not quite conform to the Kierkegaardian[8] process. It is not irony that brings about his ethical outlook upon life. His critical irony does not occasion his choice, it follows it. It is the bitter fruit of his experience of responsibility.

I have deliberately neglected a number of ironic effects, even when they are associated with dramatic development. Such is, for instance, the final conflagration which was meant to allow the capture of Ralph, but which, in fact, is the means of his deliverance. A conflagration, we remember, which was lit by those who had no wish to be rescued and refused to look after the small signal fire on the mountain top. As the ultimate manifestation of evil, that conflagration is very important indeed, but its significance does not lie in the attendant irony.

Thus I have preferred to focus my study on the irony that comes of man's infirmity, that of games that turn into war, and of action that frustrates intention. I have also analysed the irony that is to be found in the dereliction of the good intent on helping the wicked, and that which is manifest in a world over which misunderstanding holds sway jointly with the Lord of the Flies.

Golding's irony is that of a moralist who exposes aberrant conduct and multiform evil, but opens no vista into a world to which man could aspire.

8. Søren Kierkegaard, Danish religious philosopher who insisted on the need for individual decision in the search for religious truth

CHAPTER 4

Evaluation of *Lord of the Flies*

Lord of the Flies: Fiction or Fable?

John Peter

John Peter claims *Lord of the Flies* is heavy-handed.
He says that Golding is too explicit in explaining the
meaning of his fable and that he intrudes too often to
explain Simon's symbolic role. John Peter has taught
English at Cambridge University in England, the
University of Manitoba and the University of Victoria
in Canada, and the University of Wisconsin at Madi-
son. He is the author of *Complaint and Satire in
Early English Literature* and three novels: *Take
Hands at Winter, Along That Coast,* and *Runaway.*

A useful critical distinction may be drawn between a fiction
and a fable. Like most worthwhile distinctions it is often
easy to detect, less easy to define. The difficulty arises because the clearest definition would be in terms of an author's intentions, his pre-verbal procedures, and these are
largely inscrutable and wholly imprecise. For a definition
that is objective and specific we are reduced to an "as if,"
which is at best clumsy and at worst perhaps delusive.

The distinction itself seems real enough. Fables are those
narratives which leave the impression that their purpose
was anterior, some initial thesis or contention which they
are apparently concerned to embody and express in concrete terms. Fables always give the impression that they
were preceded by the conclusion which it is their function to
draw, though of course it is doubtful whether any author
foresees his conclusions as fully as this, and unlikely that his
work would be improved if he did. The effect of a fiction is
very different. Here the author's aim, as it appears from
what he has written, is evidently to present a more or less
faithful reflection of the complexities, and often of the irrel-
evancies, of life as it is actually experienced. Such conclu-

From "The Fables of William Golding" by John Peter, *Kenyon Review*, vol. 19, no. 4, Au-
tumn 1957. Copyright The Kenyon Review. Reprinted with permission.

sions as he may draw—he is under much less compulsion to draw them than a writer of fables—do not appear to be anterior but on the contrary take their origin from the fiction itself, in which they are latent, and occasionally unrecognized. It is a matter of approach, so far as that can be gauged. Fictions make only a limited attempt to generalize and explain the experience with which they deal, since their concern is normally with the uniqueness of this experience. Fables, starting from a skeletal abstract, must flesh out that abstract with the appearances of "real life" in order to render it interesting and cogent. . . .

FABLE VERSUS FICTION

Both types, the fiction and the fable, have their own particular dangers. The danger that threatens a fiction is simply that it will become confused, so richly faithful to the complexity of human existence as to lose all its shape and organization. . . . The danger that threatens a fable is utterly different, in fact the precise opposite. When a fable is poor—geometrically projected again—it is bare and diagrammatic, insufficiently clothed in its garment of actuality, and in turn its appeal is extra-aesthetic and narrow. Satires like *Animal Farm* are of this kind.

It will be said that any such distinction must be a neutral one, and that the best novels are fictions which have managed to retain their due share of the fable's coherence and order. No doubt this is true. But it also seems to be true that novels can go a good deal farther, without serious damage, in the direction of fiction than they can in the direction of fable, and this suggests that fiction is a much more congenial mode for the novelist than fable can ever be. The trouble with the mode of fable is that it is constricting. As soon as a novelist has a particular end in view the materials from which he may choose begin to shrink, and to dispose themselves toward that end. . . .

The fact is that a novelist depends ultimately not only on the richness of his materials but on the richness of his interests too; and fable, by tying these to a specific end, tends to reduce both. Even the most chaotic fiction will have some sort of emergent meaning, provided it is a full and viable reflection of the life from which it derives, if only because the unconscious preoccupations of the novelist will help to impart such meaning to it, drawing it into certain lines like iron filing sprinkled in a magnetic field. Fables, however, can only be submerged in actuality with difficulty, and they are liable to bob up again like corks, in all their plain explicitness. It may even be true to say that they are best embodied in short stories, where economy is vital and "pointlessness" (except for its brevity) comparatively intolerable.

If this is so, and creative profundity less inaccessible in fiction, why should so many modern authors prefer the mode of fable? For many do. . . . The upshot is that fable has heavily encroached on fiction in our time. Future critics, looking back, may well conclude that the best work of our generation was done in this mode, a compromise of proselytism[1] and art like the literature of the Middle Ages.

These reflections are the result of a perusal of three books by an English writer, William Golding. Their titles are *Lord of the Flies*, *The Inheritors*, and *The Two Deaths of Christopher Martin* (or *Pincher Martin*, as it was called in the English edition). All three are recent, and generally speaking all have been very well received. . . .

BOTH FICTION AND FABLE

In William Golding, *Clive Pemberton concludes that* Lord of the Flies *is fiction and fable at the same time.*

What distinguishes *Lord of the Flies* is that it is a fiction and a fable simultaneously, and if this is so, it represents a change in the nature of the novel itself. A change of a peculiarly pure nature, moreover, as it has neither been conditioned by the ruling ideas of the age nor produced in response to the literary expectations of readers.

The question of 'form' is closely related, too, to Golding's literary style, his use of words and phrases which also operate on two levels at once.

In the circumstances public praise cannot be thought to count for much; yet Golding's books are well worth the attention they have had, and rather more. On the one hand he can be taken as a diagnostic example, reflecting the interests of our time in several important ways; on the other he is a good enough writer for a preoccupation with his work not to seem precious or misdirected. Since he is not well known on

1. the practice of inducing readers to convert from one belief, cause, doctrine, or faith to another

this side of the Atlantic an introduction to his books may not be out of place.

Lord of the Flies, which appeared in 1954, is set on an imaginary South Sea island, and until the last three pages the only characters in it are boys. They have apparently been evacuated from Britain, where an atomic war is raging, and are accidentally stranded on the island without an adult supervisor. The administrative duties of their society (which includes a number of "littluns," aged about six) devolve upon their elected leader, a boy of twelve named Ralph, who is assisted by a responsible, unattractive boy called Piggy, but as time passes an independent party grows up, the "hunters," led by an angular ex–choir leader named Jack Merridew. This party, soon habituated to the shedding of animal blood, recedes farther and farther from the standards of civilization which Ralph and Piggy are straining to preserve, and before very long it is transformed into a savage group of outlaws with a costume and a ritual of their own. In the course of one of their dance-feasts, drunk with tribal excitement, they are responsible for killing the one individual on the island who has a real insight into the problems of their lives, a frail boy called Simon, subject to fainting fits, and after this more or less intentional sacrifice they lose all sense of restraint and become a band of criminal marauders, a threat to everyone on the island outside their own tribe. Piggy is murdered by their self-constituted witch-doctor and torturer, the secretive and sinister Roger, and Ralph is hunted by them across the island like the pigs they are accustomed to kill. Before they can kill and decapitate him a naval detachment arrives and takes charge of all the children who have survived.

It is obvious that this conclusion is not a concession to readers who require a happy ending—only an idiot will suppose that the book ends happily—but a deliberate device by which to throw the story into focus. With the appearance of the naval officer the bloodthirsty hunters are instantly reduced to a group of painted urchins, led by "a little boy who wore the remains of an extraordinary black cap," yet the reduction cannot expunge the knowledge of what they have done and meant to do. The abrupt return to childhood, to insignificance, underscores the argument of the narrative: that Evil is inherent in the human mind itself, whatever innocence may cloak it, ready to put forth its strength as soon as the occasion is propitious. This is Golding's theme, and it takes on a frightful force by being presented in juvenile terms, in a setting that is twice deliberately likened to the sunny Coral Island of R.M. Ballantyne. The boys' society represents, in embryo, the society of the adult world, their impulses and convictions are those of adults incisively abridged, and the whole narrative is a powerfully ironic commentary on the nature of Man, an accusation levelled at us all. There are no excuses for complacency in the fretful conscientiousness of Ralph, the leader, nor in Piggy's anxious commonsense, nor are the miscreants made to seem exceptional. When he first encounters a pig Jack Merridew is quite incapable of harming it, "because of the enormity of the knife descending and cutting into living flesh," and even the delinquent Roger is at first restrained by the taboos of "parents and school and policemen and the law." Strip these away and even Ralph might be a hunter: it is his duties as a leader that save him, rather than any intrinsic virtue in himself. Like any orthodox moralist Golding insists that Man is a fallen creature, but he refuses to hypostatize[2] Evil or to locate it in a dimension of its own. On the contrary Beëlzebub, Lord of the Flies, is Roger and Jack and you and I, ready to declare himself as soon as we permit him to.

LORD OF THE FLIES IS A FABLE

The intentness with which this thesis is developed leaves no doubt that the novel is a fable, a deliberate translation of a proposition into the dramatized terms of art, and as usual we have to ask ourselves how resourceful and complete the translation has been, how fully the thesis has been absorbed and rendered implicit in the tale as it is told. A writer of fables will heat his story at the fire of his convictions, but when he has finished the story must glow apart, generating its own heat from within. Golding himself provides a criterion for judgment here, for he offers a striking example of how complete the translation of a statement into plastic terms can be. Soon after their arrival the children develop an irrational suspicion that there is a predatory beast at large on the island. This has of course no real existence, as Piggy for one points out, but to the littluns it is almost as tangible as their castles in the sand, and most of the older boys are afraid they

2. to ascribe material existence to

may be right. One night when all are sleeping there is an air
battle ten miles above the sea and a parachuted man, already
dead, comes drifting down through the darkness, to settle
among the rocks that crown the island's only mountain.
There the corpse lies unnoticed, rising and falling with the
gusts of the wind, its harness snagged on the bushes and its
parachute distending and collapsing. When it is discovered
and the frightened boys mistake it for the beast the sequence
is natural and convincing, yet the implicit statement is quite
unmistakable too. The incomprehensible threat which has
hung over them, is, so to speak, identified and explained: a
nameless figure who is Man himself, the boys' own natures,
the something that all humans have in common.

This is finely done and needs no further comment, but
unhappily the explicit comment has already been provided,
in Simon's halting explanation of the beast's identity: "What
I mean is . . . maybe it's only us." And a little later we are told
that "However Simon thought of the beast, there rose before
his inward sight the picture of a human at once heroic and
sick." This over-explicitness is my main criticism of what is
in many ways a work of real distinction, and for two reasons
it appears to be a serious one. In the first place the fault is
precisely that which any fable is likely to incur: the incomplete translation of its thesis into its story so that much remains external and extrinsic, the teller's assertion rather
than the tale's enactment before our eyes. In the second
place the fault is a persistent one, and cannot easily be discounted or ignored. It appears in expository annotations like
this, when Ralph and Jack begin to quarrel:

> The two boys faced each other. There was the brilliant world
> of hunting, tactics, fierce exhilaration, skill; and there was
> the world of longing and baffled commonsense.

Less tolerably, it obtrudes itself in almost everything—
thought, action, and hallucination—that concerns the clair-
voyant Simon, the "batty" boy who understands "mankind's
essential illness," who knows that Ralph will get back to
where he came from, and who implausibly converses with
the Lord of the Flies. Some warrant is provided for this clair-
voyance in Simon's mysterious illness, but it is inadequate.
The boy remains unconvincing in himself, and his presence
constitutes a standing invitation to the author to avoid the
trickiest problems of his method, by commenting too baldly
on the issues he has raised. Any writer of fables must find it

hard to ignore an invitation of this kind once it exists. Golding has not been able to ignore it, and the blemishes that result impose some serious, though not decisive, limitations on a fiery and disturbing story. . . .

This brings me back, uneasily, to my original point, that fable tends to tie a writer down within his conscious purposes, restraining him, while the freedom of fiction can draw him out beyond his ascertained abilities. In view of the level of Golding's achievement, especially here, it seems futile to insist that he will never be a major novelist, but the doubt must remain to taunt an admirer like myself. Obviously a man has to write in the vein that suits him best, so that it would be impertinent, and probably destructive, to urge a maker of fables to apply himself to fictions. But it is easy to imagine some critic of the future assessing Golding's case, and deploring the conditions for literature which drove a talent so egregious into the narrow province of fable, instead of enlarging and enriching it. . . .

Judgments of this kind are not predictable, however, and in the interim work like Golding's deserves much more than casual praise. . . . Already, working in a recalcitrant mode, he seems to me to have done more for the modern British novel than any of the recent novelists who have emerged. More, it may be, than all of them.

Ranking *Lord of the Flies* as Literature

Stephen Wall

Stephen Wall attempts to rank *Lord of the Flies* among the great works of British literature published between 1930 and 1960. Though Wall concludes that Golding ranks below Irish novelist James Joyce and British novelist D.H. Lawrence, he believes Golding has made a valuable contribution to the ongoing development of the novel. In particular, he cites Golding's skill at portraying adolescent boys in *Lord of the Flies* and his ability to establish a moral position through the consciousness of these children. Stephen Wall has taught at Keble College, Oxford.

In 1930 just over 4,000 books of fiction were published in Britain; about half of these were new titles, the rest being reprints and new editions. In that year fiction formed 27 per cent of the total book production. Except for the inevitable plunge during the war of 1939–1945, the numbers of novels published annually did not fluctuate greatly during the next thirty years: there were 4,222 titles (including 2,353 reprints) in 1939: 3,871 titles (1,463 reprints) in 1951; 4,209 titles (1,820 reprints) in 1960. However, the proportion of books of fiction to the total number of published books declined steadily after the war. In 1940, they formed 34 per cent of the total; in 1950, 22 per cent; and in 1960, 18 per cent. Even so, according to the figures in *Whitaker's Cumulative Book List*, (which appears annually and from which these totals have been taken), it can be calculated that the number of new novels published during the years between 1930 and 1960 was in the region of 60,000.

THE PROCESS OF ESTABLISHING A NOVEL'S VALUE

A great many of these will have been intended as ephemeral entertainment—crime stories, adventure stories, romances,

Excerpted from "Aspects of the Novel, 1930-1960" by Stephen Wall, in *The Twentieth Century*, edited by Bernard Bergonzi, vol. 7 of History of Literature in the English Language series (London: Sphere Books, 1970). Reprinted by permission of Penguin Books, UK.

and so on—and only a small proportion of books in this category could survive literary consideration. But even a small proportion of so large a total amounts to a formidable body of respectable work, and it is obvious that no account of it can be both adequate and short. What the following pages try to offer is a brief indication of some of the qualities of a few of the novelists whose work has remained in circulation and may well survive. All the writers described in this article have contributed something distinctive to the continuing life of the novel. . . .

The volume of academic commentary on contemporary novels is now so great that instant consecration has become dangerously possible. All literary judgements, no doubt, are interim in nature, but they ought to be particularly so when the works in question have yet to demonstrate their resilience under new historical conditions and changing literary climates. When we try—as we should—to say why certain novelists are important and valuable to us in the present, we should not speak of them as if they had already taken on the established aspect of the past. It is the more important to resist any authoritarian impositions of judgement when they cannot represent the consensus of opinion over a period of time. In this article, no special legitimacy is claimed for the selection of subjects for discussion, and any local judgements made in the course of it make no pretence to finality.

As far as the heroic generation of modernism is concerned, a wide measure of agreement has of course become established: whatever one's personal attitude towards, say, Joyce[1] or D.H. Lawrence, it is accepted that they are 'there', that our literary consciousness has been deeply affected by them, that they have become, in a word, classics. That sort of status cannot yet be confidently said to belong to the novelists considered here. Few—perhaps none—of them were or are possessed of the kind of literary genius that by its nature does not occur often. Nevertheless, the best work of the novelists of this period was deeply felt and finely executed, and it justified the continuance of the novel as the dominant literary form of the time. . . .

Lord of the Flies (1954) was William Golding's first novel, and it remains his best known; indeed, its academic success

1. Irish writer James

has been extraordinary. The novel has a strong narrative appeal for young audiences, and it lends itself to interpretation with seductive ease. The fact that the doctrines which tend to emerge from the practical criticism of this text are theologically impeccable and morally wholesome makes its attractiveness, from the pedagogic point of view, all the greater. When the value of the avalanche of exegesis brought about by the educational explosion of the 1950's and 1960's comes to be considered calmly, the celebrity of *Lord of the Flies* is likely to make it a test case.

GOLDING IS UNDERRATED

In an article in the September 13, 1982, issue of the New Republic, *critic Samuel Hynes praises William Golding as England's most interesting contemporary novelist and wonders why he has been overlooked as a classic writer.*

I may as well begin with a flat proposition: I think William Golding is the most interesting English novelist now writing. I'm not sure how that proposition will strike the readers of the *New Republic*, but I'd be rather surprised if it were widely accepted; my impression is that Golding tends to be overlooked when the Novelists' League Standings are made up, as though he was known to be good, but at some other game. The rank-ordering of artists is, of course, unimportant—it's only a book reviewer's parlor game; but it is important to ask why a novelist of such extraordinary originality and power has somehow reached old age without having become an acknowledged classic. (He describes himself, wryly, as the "author of a set book"—the one novel, as all university teachers know, that every freshman can be assumed to have read.) . . .

What one feels most of all about this Man-of-Letters Golding is that though he may feel at home in Wiltshire, he is not at home in the twentieth century. Or perhaps I should put that slightly differently, and say that he is as much at home in his time as he thinks any man should be: it isn't man's fate to be at home in the world, and anyone who thinks he is doesn't understand the human condition.

Since its material and attitudes are consistent with Golding's later novels, which show an uncompromising austerity and make no concessions to easy accessibility, the wide currency of *Lord of the Flies* is in a way surprising. But among

the special factors operating in its favour is the benefit it derives from being a later variation of a myth introduced into
fiction by one of the first novels, *Robinson Crusoe*. Defoe, of
course, was immensely confident of his hero's ability to survive his isolation, and this optimism is echoed, with much
greater complacency, by the immediate source of *Lord of the
Flies*: R.M. Ballantyne's Victorian boys' story, *The Coral Island* (actually referred to on Golding's last page). Golding's
book is a refutation of Ballantyne's jolly account of the missionary fun had by his British lads on a Pacific island, but it
is still an exercise in a convention which not only children's
books show to be vigorously alive.

Ballantyne had no doubt that, even when left to their own
devices, his boy-heroes would show the moral and spiritual
soundness of their upbringing. Golding—who has been a
schoolmaster and portrays the manners and idioms of English schoolboys with great fidelity—uses his children as the
presenters of 'the end of innocence, the darkness of man's
heart', and one of the larger questions his novel provokes is
how far it is satisfactory, or simply fair, to use the potential
savagery of boys as an indication of the innate depravity of
man.

BOYS AS VEHICLES FOR A MORAL PERSPECTIVE

Although Golding himself has taken a highly allegorical
view of *Lord of the Flies*, its local, particular, and physical
life is firmly imagined. When the boys are dropped, in some
atomic holocaust, from the air onto the island, it naturally
seems to them like a dream realized; the beaches, the lagoon, the jungle have a 'strange glamour'. Ralph and Piggy
discover a shell or conch which they use to summon the others by blowing into it. Whoever holds the shell has the right
to speak at their assemblies. Much later, the destruction of
the conch accompanies the 'fall through the air' of Piggy, always the advocate of reason and science. The shell obviously becomes symbolic of those forces in the boys which
try to maintain the processes and standards of civilization.
Nevertheless, the conch is made very real as a beautiful object; Mark Kinkead-Weekes and Ian Gregor rightly remind
us that

> Physical realities come first for Golding and should stay first
> for his readers. Other meanings are found in and through
> them, as the man-breath passes through the shell-spiral to

emerge as a signal. But we must not translate the shell into the signal.

Golding is able to write virtually the whole novel in terms of the boys' consciousness because he has such a secure apprehension of those physical sensations which form so large a part of childhood experience. The boys' division into tribes, their nightmares, their taboos, their retreat behind the mask of paint, their final capitulation to the ritual of hunting that they have evolved—these retrogressive steps towards barbarism owe something to the modern study of primitive peoples, but a great deal more to the vivid factualness of both the boys and the place they find themselves in. Each step of the backward path—and much of the story's power comes from the convincing graduation from initial delight to final terror—is conveyed through the kind of experience natural to the actors. Such obvious interventions by the author as the descent onto the island of a dead parachutist (who, according to Golding. signifies 'history') are rare.

However, one character does seem under undue pressure from the novel's argument. Only Simon has the courage to face both the idol the boys have set up and the stinking corpse of the parachutist. He doesn't believe in 'the beast': 'maybe it's only us'. When he tries to bring the good news that the parachutist is not to be feared (i.e. he tries to deliver man from history), he is martyred as he cries out 'something about a body on the hill'. Simon's intense sensibility and his fainting fits help to make his religious insights plausible, but the feeling that he is 'special' because he is to a unique degree the vehicle of the novelist's doctrine remains. Simon's sea-burial, however, does show how remarkably Golding can make physical descriptions yield metaphysical implications:

> The water rose further and dressed Simon's coarse hair with brightness. The line of his cheek silvered and the turn of his shoulder became sculptured marble. The strange, attendant creatures, with their fiery eyes and trailing vapours, busied themselves round his head. The body lifted a fraction of an inch from the sand and a bubble of air escaped from the mouth with a wet plop. Then it turned gently in the water.

> Somewhere over the darkened curve of the world the sun and moon were pulling; and the film of water on the earth planet was held, bulging slightly on one side while the solid core turned. The great wave of the tide moved further along the island and the water lifted. Softly, surrounded by a fringe of inquisitive bright creatures, itself a silver shape beneath the

steadfast constellations, Simon's dead body moved out to-wards the open sea.

The sudden intrusion of the naval officer and the 'trim cruiser' at the end of *Lord of the Flies* is a shock effect de-signed to make the reader jump the gap between the boys' tragedy and the adult world.

Questioning the Literary Merit of *Lord of the Flies*

A.C. Capey

While acknowledging the widespread popularity of
Lord of the Flies with students and teachers alike,
A.C. Capey doubts that it has literary merit equal to
its popularity. Capey suggests that the novel's con-
struction allows too many interpretations. He says
that Golding presents good ideas but fails to develop
them; consequently, readers find no clear paths to
interpretation. In addition, Capey suggests that
Golding describes the boys, particularly Piggy, in
language that creates a cynical attitude and even
contempt for the boys and their tears at the end.
A.C. Capey has taught at the University of Sheffield.

It is generally assumed that *Lord of the Flies* qualifies, as do
Huckleberry Finn and *Gulliver's Travels*, for the special place
allotted to books which appeal equally to schoolchildren and
adults, teachers and scholars; and a vast interpretative in-
dustry, based on the assumption and cementing it, has
grown up, to the exclusion of 'criticism's primary task, that
of telling us whether the work of art under consideration is
any good or not' [according to Roy Fuller].

MANY MEANINGS POSSIBLE

In defence of the interpreters, they have been given a clear
invitation to quarry for meanings. 'Lord of the flies' may be
a direct translation of 'Beelzebub', but his identity in the
book is not so precise. The pig's head, swarming with flies,
is their lord, but only in an inverted way. The pig's head,
symbolically, is lord of the hunters in that they have raised
it in the spirit of crucifiers. It is ironically lord of the hunters
in so far as the boys are governed by blood-lust. But is not

Excerpted from "'Will' and 'Idea' in *Lord of the Flies*" by A.C. Capey, *Use of English*,
vol. 24, Winter 1972. Reprinted by permission of Scottish Academic Press.

Jack also lord of the flies, and was not Ralph lord originally? Between Ralph's spell of leadership and Jack's the fear of the unknown beast develops, and the dead parachutist, embodiment of the imaginary beast, restricts the activity of the boys until he is swept out to sea. If the parachutist-beast is lord, is not Simon, the sacrificial victim, also? And when the boys, giving rein to blood-lust, murder and arson, are finally out of control, the arrival of the smart naval officer represents authority over the humiliated, weeping gang on the beach— authority which is then delegated, as it were, with the question: 'Who's boss here?'

The plausibility of such interpretations has led to the assumption that the author's imagination is exercised pervasively and that the significance of the title penetrates the whole book. As a schoolmaster, I had no lack of good essays on 'Who is the lord of the flies?'. But in fact the question does not go far enough. What we are given in the variety of plausible significances is not an imaginative development of a theme but intellectually imposed alterations or alternatives of 'significance'; the ideas sit on the narrative, unassimilated. 'A chaotic kind of individualism in which anybody can read or ignore anything they like, any two opinions are democratically equal, [because they can be made plausibly to correspond] to the work being discussed' [according to D.W. Harding], appears to be invited. Mr. Golding is playing a game with us, and when (as in his American lecture, 1962) he stops playing it and steps in to direct the lines of inquiry, we are forced to choose between following his limiting lead and breaking our 'bond with the author':

> My book was to say: you think that now the war is over and an evil thing destroyed, you are safe because you are naturally kind and decent. But I know why the thing rose in Germany. I know it could happen in any country. It could happen here.

> So the boys try to construct a civilisation on the island; but it breaks down in blood and terror because the boys are suffering from the terrible disease of being human ('Fable', *The Hot Gates*).

That there is no 'lord of the flies' but only the beast which is within us is offered as Simon's discovery, and fully realised in Simon's death, when in attempting to impart his knowledge to the others he 'becomes the beast':

> The beast was on its knees in the centre, its arms folded over its face. It was crying out against the abominable noise some-

thing about a body on the hill. The beast struggled forward, broke the ring and fell over the steep edge of the rock to the sand by the water. At once the crowd surged after it, poured down the rock, leapt on to the beast, screamed, struck, bit, tore. There were no words, and no movements but the tearing of teeth and claws.

In responding to the artistic creation there we register the selflessness of Simon, the hysterical fury of the boys' assault on the 'thing' that 'came darkly, uncertainly . . . out of the forest', and the irony of their mistake; and we register the further irony that in mistaking or substituting Simon for the beast the boys are transformed into beasts themselves, thereby enacting the knowledge of 'the terrible disease of being human' that Simon has come to give them. But the imaginative effect is, for Mr. Golding, only the sugar on the pill. A writer who could trust his tale to dramatise the meaning would not have inserted the information about 'a body on the hill'. The hysterical boys, as imaginatively presented, have no ears for words, nor as they move in for the kill do they utter any; the distinguishing mark of the human being has been eliminated. But Mr. Golding, concerned as fabulist and moralist to tuck 'a human lesson . . . away' in the language of incident and description, has to tell the reader what Simon has come to say—has to maintain the overtly significant connexion with the fruits of Simon's lone expedition to the heart of the matter.

IDEAS LACK CLEAR DEVELOPMENT

The interpreters, aided and abetted by the author, ascribe more precise significance to Simon. Simon is a saint, a Christ-figure, helping the littl'uns, alone in the wilderness tempted of the Devil, removing the dead body of history ('the past . . . [which] won't lie down' is Mr. Golding's explanation of Simon's perception that 'the beast was harmless and horrible'), and 'embracing [his] fate'. 'It was worked out very carefully in every possible way, this novel,' Mr. Golding assures us. The only question to concern us, however, is whether the Christ-figure is realised imaginatively; if the message has to be decoded it isn't there. A momentary assimilation of Simon with Christ is apparent in the sacrifice, despite the author's disclaimer: 'He who was without sin became sin for us' comes to mind once the idea of the Christ-figure is given us. But for the most part the ideas bob around at odds with the narrative. . . .

Mr. Golding habitually presents an idea and discards it; no thematic thought develops it or gives it the resonance required for it to be more than an idea. The clue to Ralph's return is given here, with an insistence we cannot ignore; but there is no substance in the character of Simon or in Ralph's memories of his pleasant home or in the general behaviour of the boys (their failure to keep the fire alight, for example) to give imaginative support to the clue, which remains an undigested assertion, 'carefully worked in'. . . .

The Fall of Man is the principal explicit idea in *Lord of the Flies.* Ralph at the end

> had a fleeting picture of the strange glamour that had once invested the beaches . . . 'We were together then' . . . Ralph wept for the end of innocence, the darkness of man's heart, and the fall through the air of the true, wise friend called Piggy.

But Ralph and the author are deceiving themselves. That the island, now scorched, was originally glamorous is true; 'glamour' occurs frequently in the early part of the book and the first expedition shows exhilaration:

> A kind of glamour was spread over them and the scene and they were conscious of the glamour and made happy by it. They turned to each other, laughing excitedly, talking, not listening. The air was bright.

But Piggy has just been snubbed, and the potential rivalry between Ralph and Jack has appeared. If the boys at first are co-operative and clean and know not the doctrine of ill-doing, they are yet already potentially dirty and cruel. The fall of the passenger tube from the burning aircraft has exacted its metaphorical significance. The orderly choir, still dutiful, is swaying in the heat and will not be referred to as the choir for much longer. There are thorns on the island, and the first thing we learn about the fruit is that it induces diarrhoea. The author from the start is creatively bent away from the paradisial features, despite the place he accords them. The conch's power is a childish rule or invention; the littl'uns fall off the parliamentary log; and even the first meeting breaks up with more enthusiasm than it begins. Alongside the selfless activity of Simon and his appreciation of the incense-bearing trees we have Roger, who hides a dark soul and foul thoughts and is restrained from throwing stones at Henry only by the too recent memory of adult sanctions. The author, having pre-determined that any resemblance to the civilised structures of *The Coral Island* shall be 'realistic', is unable to create the paradise his fable requires. It is no accident that 'glamour', a superficial notion, should persistently be used of the paradisial features.

The truth is that the author despises the boys. 'I have lived for many years with small boys,' he says, 'and understand and know them with awful precision'. But his knowledge and understanding are tarnished by cynicism, the product of a limited vision of human nature, a partial view of history and a schoolmasterish tendency to denigrate children. Cynical contempt appears time and again in the novel, characteristically in the form of gratuitous judgment by an adult observer. 'Let's have a vote,' the boys cry at the first meeting, 'Vote for chief!'—and the sour comment follows:

> This toy of voting was almost as pleasing as the conch... None of the boys could have found good reason for [an election by acclaim of Ralph]; what intelligence had been shown was traceable to Piggy.

After the preliminary expedition to discover the limits of the island, 'the three boys [begin] to scramble up' the mountain and have to contend with entangling creepers. Not content with recording their *Beano*-style ejaculations—'Wacco', 'Wizard', 'Smashing'—the author obtrudes avuncular disenchantment: 'The cause of their pleasure was not obvious.' Of the same order is this reductive comment on Ralph, at a point when he is about to show concern for others and thoughtful leadership; darkness is coming down, and the hunt for the beast has lost its way:

> By now, Ralph had no self-consciousness in public thinking but would treat the day's decisions as though he were playing chess. The only trouble was that he would never be a very good chess player.

There is too something overwhelmingly cynical in the way the boys, as things go wrong, are shown turning to the absent adults for support. As a mirror of adult society *Lord of the Flies* is devised to reflect the disintegration of Mr. Golding's world; the adults can offer no hope.

> 'If only they could get a message to us,' cried Ralph desperately. 'If only they could send us something grown-up... a sign or something.'

Cynicism and contempt override the legitimate despair in the sequel:

> A thin wail out of the darkness chilled them and set them

grabbing for each other. Then the wail rose, remote and un-earthly, and turned to an inarticulate gibbering. Percival Wemys Madison, of the vicarage, Harcourt St. Anthony, lying in the long grass, was living through circumstances in which the incantation of his address was powerless to help him.

—The incantation there, inexcusably, is the author's.

GOLDING BELITTLES PIGGY

Piggy, to whom Mr. Golding ascribes intelligence after the example of *Animal Farm,* comes in for his share of denigra-tion, in the accents of the author as well as the boys'. When the 'errant assembly' first follows Jack up the mountain to make a fire, Piggy wears 'the martyred expression of a parent who has to keep up with the senseless ebullience of the chil-dren'. When 'land loomed where there was no land and flicked out like a bubble as the children watched, ... Piggy discounted all this learnedly as a "mirage"'. When, in the final confrontation between sense and savagery, Roger's rock

> struck Piggy a glancing blow from chin to knee ... [and] Piggy, saying nothing, with no time for even a grunt, travelled through the air sideways from the rock, turning over as he went, ... [to fall] forty feet and [land] on his back across that square, red rock in the sea ... ,

the impressive description is marred by the betraying phrase: 'with no time for even a grunt'. The author's inser-tion is destructive—destructive of the seriousness with which we are subsequently asked to take 'the fall through the air of the true, wise friend called Piggy', as well as of Piggy's moral status. When Roger sharpens a stick at both ends, in order presumably to impale Ralph's head as he has earlier impaled the pig's, we are moved to reflect that Mr. Golding's stick is often similarly sharpened. Piggy is made to die a double death. ...

The power of Mr. Golding's art depends also upon the show—the shown significance of the 'grunt' (which 'means' more than the author's clever sneer), the smashed conch and the spilt brains:

> ... the conch exploded into a thousand white fragments and ceased to exist ... [Piggy's] head opened and stuff came out.

The alert pupil is expected to register through those carefully presented symbols the ultimate fragility of the boys' tenuous grasp on sense, order and legitimate behaviour. That the falling Piggy, representative of intelligence and the rule of law, is an unsatisfactory symbol of fallen man seems not to worry Mr. Golding, whose willed insistence on administering the pill and leaving the sugar to look after itself—*who* hears the grunt or sees the conch disintegrate?—exposes his art as the incoherently conscious thing it is.

The same point, finally, must be made of the rescue. There *is* a happy ending to *Lord of the Flies,* and it is contained in the fulfilment of Simon's promise: Ralph will return to where he came from. The irony of the successful smoke-signal seems to me much more germane to the tensions and quarrels of the book than the imposed idea, in the last sentence, that the boys have merely been doing in their small corner what the adults are doing in the world at large. The idea—perfectly in accord with Mr. Golding's *scheme*—in fact constitutes a snub to the children's tears of mortification and relief.

The morally and artistically disabling idea governing Mr. Golding's fiction hardly qualifies as 'thought'—indeed the author has himself disclaimed any thought on the Fall beyond its topical manifestation in war and mass-murder. Yet for all its limitations, or perhaps because of them, *Lord of the Flies* has become an educational institution, widely taught on both sides of the Atlantic. Mr. Golding put a lot of 'careful work' into devising the programme, laying the trail and placing the clues, almost as if he were concocting the most eminently teachable book of our time. And certainly it offers ample scope for classroom activity, essay-titles and examination questions: its superficial coherence allows pupils given 'The significance of the conch or Piggy's spectacles' to range over the whole book. Whether such matters approach the central critical issues is doubtful, however; and I suggest that the teachability rather than any clearly established merit of the book is responsible for the general acclaim with which it has been received.

The Unwarranted Popularity of *Lord of the Flies*

R.C. Townsend

R.C. Townsend argues that the premise of *Lord of the Flies* is faulty and that Golding manipulates readers into accepting the error. According to Townsend, the book wrongly concludes that humans are no more than beasts, that evil is inherent in human nature. Townsend argues that Golding consistently intrudes into the narrative to persuade readers to think his way. He also says that the ending is weak: The rescue means Golding avoids carrying his argument to its logical conclusion and leaves readers in confusion. American critic R.C. Townsend has written numerous journal articles, several for the general reader.

The rise of William Golding's *Lord of the Flies* to the top of best-seller and required reading lists should suggest to the teacher of literature and the social sciences important insights into his students', and perhaps his own, willingness to be taken in by false profundity and false art. When the book was first published in 1954 it had an interestingly mixed reception. Reviewers sensed that it was by no means flawless, but they retreated from literary grounds and ended up praising or condemning the book on the basis of their agreement or disagreement with Golding's thesis about what lies beneath the thin veneer of civilization. "The fantasy comes too close to reality," the reviewer for the *New York Times* wrote, "if criticism must be leveled at such a feat of the imagination, it is permissible to carp at the very premise on which the whole strange story is founded." English reviewers were, on the whole, not awed (Walter Allen, for example, pointed out that it was "only a rather unpleasant and too-easily affecting story"); American reviewers either turned away ("well-

Excerpted from *"Lord of the Flies: Fool's Gold?"* by R.C. Townsend, *Journal of General Education*, vol. 26, April 1964-January 1965, pp. 153-60. Copyright 1965 by The Pennsylvania State University. Reproduced by permission of The Pennsylvania State University Press.

written but completely unpleasant story," said the *New Yorker*) or, like the *New York Herald Tribune* reviewer, got drawn in: "too many nagging questions remain unanswered, but the magic of a born story-teller makes us forget our reservations, and *Lord of the Flies*, engrossing from the first page, winds up being almost too persuasive."

The present enthusiasm for Golding's book in America dates back primarily to 1959 when it was reissued in a paperback edition. . . . In January 1962 the book review section of the *New York Times* began to carry accounts of the novel's race to the popularity it now enjoys: "In the Ivy League, at any rate, William Golding's *Lord of the Flies* is edging up on Salinger." Seven months later another reviewer looked out upon a less exclusive scene and found that it "has been pressing J.D. Salinger's work in popularity, particularly among students, running a close second to *Catcher in the Rye* in campus bookstores." Two months after that yet another reviewer wrote: "William Golding's grim comment on the human race, *Lord of the Flies*, is . . . fast overtaking J.D. Salinger's *Catcher in the Rye* in the affections of students on eastern college campuses." By the time the newspaper strike was over the race was won; the *Times* announced that *Lord of the Flies* had become the best-selling paperback in America. . . .

The *New Republic* invited "faculty members of four universities to account for this popularity" and only one told of (or shared) the dissatisfaction of some students with the novel's "pretentiousness, obviousness, and oversimplification." A film has been made of it and in a cozy advertisement in the *New Yorker* the producers and the director describe what is the usual response: "it has become required reading in schools, and is the unchallenged darling of the sensitive literati." Because this is so, another look at *Lord of the Flies* can help us not only to judge the book but also to suggest some things about the malleability of students, teachers, and other "literati.". . .

CRITICISM OF THE THESIS AND THE TREATMENT

Presumably one starts with the hope—if not the belief—that Golding's thesis is wrong, that finally man is more than a beast, but to object to the book on these grounds is to make the mistake of the first reviewers. Yet it is understandable why they retreated to the "very premise" on which the story is based; at least that is just where Golding wants to engage

his reader, and on first reading the book one is more concerned about Piggy's glasses or Ralph's rescue than about
how Golding is luring his reader up a path which leads only
to an acceptance of his thesis. But after a second reading it
becomes clear how unsure Golding is of that thesis and of
his ability to make his fable suggest it. He thinks he would
be unable (or he knows we would be unwilling) to move
from the terms of one to those of the other and so he contin-
ually makes the jump for us.

LORD OF THE FLIES IS MEANINGLESS

In the October 15, 1955, issue of Saturday Review of Literature, *Louis J. Halle concludes that Golding's novel does nothing more than identify the conflict between civilization and
savagery.*

Civilization had come down out of the sky with the
children.
But so had savagery, and fear of the unknown brought it
out. . . . So the struggle between civilization and barbarism
began.
William Golding tells all this in his first novel, *Lord of the
Flies.* One is impressed by the possibilities of his theme for
an expression of the irony and tragedy of man's fate. Against
his majority of little savages he places a remnant that con-
vincingly represents the saving element of human heroism,
thereby posing the eternal moral conflict. But he cannot
quite find his meaning in this material. The heroes come to
a bad end, having contributed nothing to such salvation as
the society achieves. There is a great deal of commotion,
and the last page is nothing more than a playwright's con-
trivance for bringing down the curtain. One is left asking:
What was the point?

Thus Ralph and Jack become, he tells us, "two continents
of experience and feeling, unable to communicate" and are
later opposed as "the brilliant world of hunting, tactics,
fierce exhilaration, skill" and the "world of longing and baffled commonsense." Piggy, the most intelligent of the boys
and the possessor of the only recognizable voice in the novel
(though ironically because of his bad grammar) looks into
the fire and, it is claimed, "glanced nervously into hell." At
one point Simon tries "to express man's essential illness,"
and the eyes of the pig's head into which he gazes are "dim

with the infinite cynicism of adult life"; at another point Sam and Eric protest, Golding says, "out of the heart of civilization." And on the final page, as is well known, the cause of Ralph's tears is supposed to be "the end of innocence, the darkness of man's heart." It is as if Aesop had told us that the fox really liked grapes but was calling them sour because he was unable to reach them.

But Aesop was clear about the separation of his fable and his moral, and consequently so are we. He does not expect the fox's hunger pains to upset us; we can go on to join him in his conclusions about man's rationalizations. But we do care about children's hunger pains and about bullying, and realizing this, Golding is quick to name our concern as one for "mankind's essential illness." He does not trust us to move from the terms of one to those of the other, so he forces children into moral positions and attitudes they could never take and that he could not come out and make explicit in the novel itself. . . .

EXPLOITING CHARACTERS AND STUDENTS

In objecting to what Golding is doing in *Lord of the Flies* there is no need to invoke Jamesian principles about intrusive narrators or more modern edicts about impersonality. Golding is obviously violating these, but we are learning not to rely too heavily on them and he is doing much more. For not only is he exploiting Ralph and Piggy and Simon but he is also exploiting the thousands of students who are committed to the book. Carried along by the excitement of a first reading it is not clear where the voice is coming from (thus Walter Allen's nice phrase, "too easily affecting"). If Simon is trying to "express mankind's essential illness," it may seem plausible that we don't amount to much after all, that the effort isn't really worth it. It is an age in which the voice of despair is particularly seductive to the ears of a student, so Golding's easy cynicism usually goes unchallenged. And it is no more than "easy cynicism." That reference to "the infinite cynicism of adult life" need apply to no one else but to him. "When I was young, before the war," he said breezily in a recent *New Republic* interview, "I did have some airy-fairy views about man . . . But I went through the war and that changed me. The war taught me different and a lot of others like me." Students are also willing to be "taught different"; indeed, Golding once admitted that they have "a vague sense" (only "a vague sense" unfortunately) that "he too has it in for the whole world of organization."

One might account for the popularity of *Lord of the Flies* only in terms of Golding's exploitation of student bewilderment, but teachers of literature and political science, and, conceivably, "anthropologists, social psychologists and philosophical historians . . ." have contributed greatly. It is they, after all, who assign the book and it seems that the book was first read (and still is read) as "required reading." It would be too harsh to say that they also "have it in for the whole world of organization," but though they may not be looking for prophecies of doom they are all too eager to find some sort of significant statement or some symbolic use of language. And so a facile comment on the human condition is heard as an apocalyptic voice. Should the ear need convincing, there is the students' eager acceptance of the book; should the teaching of the book need some justification or some "tone," there is all that Symbolism—conch, glasses, parachutist, or the lord of the flies who "is, of course, a translation of the Hebrew. . . ." The book is eminently teachable: it "speaks to students," the symbolism can be "worked out." But what does not get demonstrated, apparently, is that in order to force its dubious conclusions upon us the voice that speaks relies not on any authority it possesses but on our inattention, and that Golding's symbolism emanates from a desire to support the conclusions rather than from a total commitment to his subject, whether that subject be defined as the fate of a handful of boys after a nuclear attack or the defects of society and human nature. . . .

At the end of *Lord of the Flies*, on the other hand, a caricature of a British naval officer (i.e., civilization) rescues the boys, and barbarous Jack does not protest fair-haired Ralph's assertion that he is their leader. One critic has read the ending as an indication that "civilization defeats the beast"; another asserts that "only an idiot will suppose that the book ends happily" and defends the ending as "a deliberate device by which to throw the story into focus," a device by which Golding "underscores the argument of the narrative: that Evil is inherent in the human mind itself, whatever innocence may cloak it." Yes, we may step back and wonder at the thinness of the cloak, but we are still relieved that the book ends, if not happily, at least far less unhappily than it might have had Golding either carried its fable out to the conclusion that would be most natural to it or followed the implications of his thesis to the end. And we are also left wondering: if it takes no more than that to reestablish the world of organization, is the darkness not so powerful after all? or is Golding unable to face the implications of the thesis he has flirted with throughout the novel? We do see that once again Golding has manipulated his fable arbitrarily. Whether it be to support his thesis indirectly or to avoid its implications is not of primary importance. What is of primary importance is that he has used a delicate subject in this way and that thousands of readers have been been used in their turn.

Assessing
Lord of the Flies

Frederick R. Karl

Frederick R. Karl's 1961 evaluation of *Lord of the Flies* praises Golding for experimenting with the novel and imagining human behavior without the inhibitions of society. He does, however, identify flaws in Golding's execution of these ideas. In particular, Karl cites the rescue as a gimmick and criticizes Golding's tendency to moralize. Karl's 1972 reevaluation is more critical. Comparing *Lord of the Flies* with Joseph Conrad's *Heart of Darkness*, which addresses the same theme, Karl says that Golding fails to illuminate the paradoxes of both civilization and savagery. Unlike *Heart of Darkness*, *Lord of the Flies* lacks the depth, according to Karl, that makes a work worth revisiting over time. Frederick R. Karl taught English at New York University. He has written books on novelists Joseph Conrad, William Faulkner, and Franz Kafka and is the author of *The Contemporary English Novel* and *A Century of Fiction: The British Novel in the Nineteenth Century*.

There is little question of William Golding's originality as a novelist. He has not been afraid to experiment with form or to attempt daring themes: for instance, life amid a predatory group of stranded boys in *Lord of the Flies*, 1954; the decline and death of man's immediate predecessors on earth, in *The Inheritors*, 1955; the struggle for survival of a shipwrecked sailor, in *The Two Deaths of Christopher Martin* (in England, *Pincher Martin*), 1956; a man's attempt to trace his guilt and his subsequent fall from grace, in *Free Fall*, 1959. In each of the novels, the manner is indirect, the symbols rarely clarified, and the method of narration uncondescending and stringent. Golding is obviously striving to move behind the

From "The Novel as Moral Allegory: The Fiction of William Golding, Iris Murdoch, Rex Warner, and P.H. Newby; Postscript: 1960-1970" by Frederick R. Karl, in *A Reader's Guide to the Contemporary English Novel* by Frederick R. Karl. Copyright ©1960 by Frederick R. Karl. Copyright © renewed 1987 by Frederick R. Karl. Reprinted by permission of Farrar, Straus & Giroux, Inc.

conventional matter of the contemporary novel to a view of what man, or pre-man, is really like when his facade of civilized behavior falls away.

Like Graham Greene in his religious novels, Golding is interested in the metaphysics of behavior. He is not simply a social novelist attempting to see man's response to a given society, but a metaphysical writer interested in states of being and aspects of survival. . . . Golding is interested not in the superficial capabilities of man but in those long-buried responses the latter can suddenly evoke in order to satisfy or preserve himself. It is not surprising that three of Golding's four novels are directly concerned with man's struggle for survival, with his attempt to maintain not only body but also soul. For under these circumstances, man loses his superficial social mask and becomes man reduced to any course that will insure his life. . . .

PRIMITIVE SAVAGERY EMERGES

As in Greene's novels, there are beliefs and values operating in Golding's fiction that must dominate despite the main thrust of each novel toward disbelief. For most of his narrative, he seems to be concerned with moral aimlessness: the stranded boys in *Lord of the Flies*, for example, almost entirely shake off their civilized behavior. Under certain conditions of survival, the primitive element predominates; residual savagery lies barely below the surface and is controlled only under the right circumstances. Remove these circumstances and the boys are amoral, vicious, chaotic, murderous. What Golding senses is that institutions and order imposed from without are temporary, but that man's irrationality and urge for destruction are enduring.

The stranded boys under Ralph's leadership divide into two groups, those who will supply the food and those who will keep the fire, their only hope of attracting attention. In a way, the fire-keepers are the poets, the contemplative ones, while the hunters are the doers, the men of action. As in the real world, so here, the hunters begin to woo the fire-keepers, for to do is more glamorous than to be. Having first aimed at their common salvation, the two groups soon divide into warring factions. Ralph, however, possesses the conch shell (a symbol of his "poetic" power), which attracts some of the boys to his side, but even that piece of magic is eventually destroyed when the hunters become violent.

Physical force comes to smother magic, religion, creativity, humanity itself.

The boys become caught by the chaos of violence and its accompanying quality: fear. They begin to stalk Ralph across the island, and they viciously attack and kill Simon when he comes to tell them of a rotting skeleton at which the lord of the flies has picked away. As the skeleton has been eaten, so is Simon, in a kind of ritualistic death, torn to pieces by boys screaming *"Kill the beast! Cut his throat! Spill his blood."* The blood thirst of their chant has poked through the veneer of civilization, and they are helpless within the throes of a primitive passion.

Finally, a rescue force comes to the island before Ralph is killed, and the boys are chided by the officer in charge for their failure to put up a better show. The officers themselves are engaged in an atomic attack of some sort, and the implication is that while the adults are disappointed by the boys the former are themselves of course little better. Ralph himself is torn by tears which indicate that his childhood and innocence are gone forever, that he has been initiated into a malevolent adult world from which escape is impossible. Crying for a childhood lost beyond redemption, he recognizes through his tears what he must face for the rest of his life.

Structural Faults Diminish a Powerful Theme

When the boys on the island struggle for supremacy, they reenact a ritual of the adult world. . . . Golding, by treating the boys' imagination as childish, dilutes the seriousness of the theme. Without gaining the possible irony he intended, he partially dissipates the tremendous force of his narrative; the power that conflicting passions have generated dribbles away in the resolution.

There is in all of Golding's work this crucial avoidance of subtlety, and that is perhaps why his novels are concerned almost solely with primitive struggles for survival. . . . The boys become semi-civilized, and consequently they converse and act at a level that precludes mature thought. Once the originality of the allegory and language wears off, we see merely a number of semi-articulate boys having a savage romp.

The idea of a Golding novel invariably is superior to the performance itself. Ironically, the idea, often so engaging in the abstract, is self-defeating, for it forces an artificial method. Golding is an allegorist whose allegory preempts the realistic level; often, only the allegory is of interest and when that begins to wear thin, there is insufficient substance to grapple with.

Golding's novels, then, seem more attractive in their parts than as wholes. His inability, or lack of desire, to give intellectual substance to his themes, and his didactic intrusion in nearly all of the narratives, lessen the power of what still remains, however, an original talent. His eccentric themes, unfortunately, rarely convey the sense of balance and ripeness that indicate literary maturity. . . . Stranded boys are compelling only if their behavior indicates something significant about them and not merely their similarity to adults. . . . To present all of these characters and situations "straight" is to take them as they are, and this evaluation simplifies them all out of proportion to what Golding's serious intentions demand.

To end a discussion of Golding's work on this note is, however, to lose sight of his importance to the contemporary novel. Even if his didacticism[1] makes him resolve what should be unresolvable, he nevertheless indicates in nearly every line that he is an artist seriously interested in his craft. And even if he seems prone to surprise the reader with gimmicks, he nevertheless has demonstrated a sharp enough awareness of his material to overcome this defect before it permanently damages his fiction. When literary values overcome the moralist, Golding's potential may well be realized, and he will become an outstanding novelist.

•   •   •   •   •

Since Golding's work in the previous decade has slackened, it may be time to take another look at *Lord of the Flies,* which is now seventeen years old. No English writer of the last generation has been as closely identified with a single book, and in America only Salinger's *Catcher in the Rye* comes to mind as a comparable phenomenon. Yet the Salinger book has not held up well over the years; Holden has proven too innocent, too romantic, ultimately too much an American Adam. Must we say the same of the Golding novel —that after a decade of acclaim by academic critics, its psychological apparatus no longer engages the mature reader? That despite its evident concern with evil, despite its broad allegorical implications, despite its often striking lyricism of phrase and scene, despite

1. moral, ethical, or religious guidance in a literary work

Golding's ability to create a distinct world—that despite all these obvious virtues, the novel does not extend beyond itself and become wedged into our consciousness? Or can we say that it fills out enough of its own myth so that, like *Robinson Crusoe* and *Heart of Darkness*, it generates a power that goes beyond word and phrase?

GOLDING AND CONRAD EXPLORE SIMILAR THEMES

One of the chief difficulties is, of course, that no single character obtrudes. The counter-argument would be that the island, or the isolated situation itself, is the chief character; but what goes on is too full of people not to produce a protagonist. Furthermore, a book fathering only children has its problems when it attempts to move beyond a children's world. Ideologically, *Lord of the Flies* and *Heart of Darkness* are analogous, and in that comparison perhaps we can see why one remains in a minor genre while the other works for each new generation. We remember that in 1962 Golding said he had never read *Heart of Darkness*, but read it or not, he is treading on Conrad's territory, not only in *Lord of the Flies* but throughout his entire canon.

The essential basis for comparison is that both Golding and Conrad interested themselves in situations that offer no other restraint except what the self may provide. Somewhere one must find it, and it is an individual, not a social, matter. Restraint is a muscular courage not to do, and it marks the difference between civilization and capitulation to savagery. Yet where does it come from? How does one obtain it, especially if it is innate and not social? Conrad's chief example of someone lacking restraint is Kurtz: he goes to the Congo as a missionary and his final solution for the savage is to kill him. It is Conrad's irony that Kurtz is doing the world's dirty work and represents not barbarism but the forces of civilization.

Golding's children, except for Ralph, Simon, and Piggy, become barbaric like Kurtz, reverting to a level of savage behavior that pokes through their civilized veneer. The boys undergo considerable loss of restraint, at the same time gaining some consciousness of their debasement. If Golding had left it at that, he might have had a symbolic action of some magnitude. But the deus ex machina[2] of naval officers

2. the employment of an improbable or unexpected event in a story to make things turn out right

saves Ralph from the pack and the pack itself from the fire; this changes all the terms. For with the officers, Golding is saying that the adult world offers the safeguards of civilization, that those officers, with their spotless uniforms and their spick-and-span cruiser, offer an alternative to the boys, who had "let go." Thus restraint is still possible, and it is British; one had simply expected better behavior of the boys.

Conrad had avoided this very point. If restraint or the lack of it is to be taken seriously—and that is a dubious proposition to begin with—then it cannot first be questioned in boys only to be demonstrated in adults. The quality either exists or does not exist. Golding resolves the entire question by falling back on British civilization; while Conrad's Marlow, much chastened, much tempted, almost seduced, goes back to preserve civilization with a lie. Golding has reduced his situation to a preachment, to the effect that these boys have grown up. Ralph weeps for his loss of innocence and for the fall of Piggy and man; but Marlow's lies about himself and about Kurtz are too deep-seated for tears. They embody ironies and paradoxes for which there is no explanation, and they permeate everywhere as a condition of both civilization and savagery. Golding has made the situation into games, savage though they are, while Conrad would suggest that naval officers commit their own brand of atrocities.

Possibly *Lord of the Flies* has been so well received by students because it seems to offer a paradigm[3] of the adult world; but it does no such thing. In Golding's terms, the adult world is a hedge against what the children experience in themselves, and therefore those who read the book seeking a broader statement are bound to be disappointed. A complacent Christian morality hangs heavy on the novel, from the choir boys' doffing of their robes decorated with crosses to Jack's tears of repentance and the gaining of self-knowledge. Golding wants to show that evil lurks beneath smooth surfaces, ready to poke out, not to make a social or political point about children and from them about the adult world. This is another way of saying that Golding's concern with moral issues, with the secular fall from grace, never approaches the intensity of *Heart of Darkness*.

3. an example that serves as a pattern or a model

CHRONOLOGY

1901

Queen Victoria dies

1903

Wright brothers make first successful airplane flight at Kitty Hawk

1905

Einstein publishes special theory of relativity

1911

William Golding born in St. Columb Minor, Cornwall

1912

Women protest for the right to vote; the *Titanic* sinks

1914

World War I begins in Europe

1917

U.S. enters World War I; Golding enters Marlborough Grammar School

1919

Treaty of Versailles, ending World War I

1920

League of Nations established

1929

New York Stock Exchange Crash; beginning of Great Depression

1930

Golding graduates from Marlborough; enters Brasnose College, Oxford

1933

Hitler becomes chancellor of Germany; the Dust Bowl prompts westward migration in U.S.

1934

Poems published

1935–1939

Golding works as social worker and in small theaters

1935

Golding receives B.A. in English and a diploma in education from Oxford

1936

Outbreak of Spanish Civil War

1939

Golding marries Ann Brookfield; begins teaching English and philosophy at Bishop Wordsworth's School in Salisbury, Wiltshire; Spanish Civil War ends; World War II begins

1940

Golding joins Royal Navy; Winston Churchill becomes prime minister

1941

Germany invades Russia; Japanese attack Pearl Harbor; U.S. enters World War II

1942

Hitler begins extermination of European Jews

1944

D day: Allies invade France; Franklin D. Roosevelt elected to fourth term as president

1945

U.S. drops atomic bombs on cities in Japan; Japan surrenders; World War II ends; Golding returns to Bishop Wordsworth's School; Nuremberg trials

1946

First assembly of United Nations

1947

Beginning of the Marshall Plan; India gains independence from Britain

1948

Mahatma Gandhi assassinated; Russians blockade Berlin

1949

Communist government in China; North Atlantic Treaty Organization (NATO) established

1950

Korean War begins

1953

Death of Stalin; end of Korean War

1954

Lord of the Flies published; Elvis Presley releases first record, beginning of rock music

1955

The Inheritors published

1956

Pincher Martin published in England; published in U.S. as *The Two Lives of Christopher Martin* in 1957

1957

Russia launches *Sputnik*

1958

The Brass Butterfly, a play, published and performed

1959

Free Fall published; Castro takes power in Cuba

1960

Miss Pulkinhorn, a radio play, airs

1960–1962

Golding reviews books for the *Spectator*

1961

Break My Heart, a radio play, airs; Golding completes master of arts degree at Oxford; leaves teaching; Berlin Wall seals Iron Curtain; Soviet cosmonaut is first man to orbit earth

1961–1962

Golding is a writer in residence at Hollins College, Virginia; lecture tour of other American colleges

1963

President John F. Kennedy assassinated

1964

The Spire published

1965

Golding awarded OBE, Commander, Order of the British Empire

1966

Hot Gates and Other Occasional Pieces, a book of essays, published; Golding becomes honorary fellow of Brasenose College, Oxford

1967

The Pyramid published; Christiaan Barnard performs first human heart transplant

1968

Robert Kennedy and Martin Luther King assassinated

1970

Golding awarded doctor of letters by Sussex University

1971

The Scorpion God published

1972

U.S. Apollo astronauts land on the moon

1973

Vietnam War cease-fire agreement signed

1974

Richard Nixon resigns and Gerald Ford becomes president of U.S.

1976

Mao Tse-tung, chairman of Chinese Communist Party, dies

1979

Darkness Visible published; Margaret Thatcher becomes British prime minister

1980

Rites of Passage published and wins Booker McConnell Prize for best novel of the year

1981

Prince Charles marries Lady Diana Spencer

1982

A Moving Target, a book of essays, published; Falkland Islands War between Great Britain and Argentina

1983

Golding is awarded the Nobel Prize in literature

1984

The Paper Men published

1985

An Egyptian Journal, a record of Golding's travels, published

1987

Close Quarters published

1989

Fire Down Below published; Berlin Wall is torn down after twenty-eight years

1991

Gulf War to stop Iraq's invasion of Kuwait; dismantling of the Soviet Union

1992

Civil war begins in Bosnia

1993

Golding dies June 19

FOR FURTHER RESEARCH

ABOUT WILLIAM GOLDING AND *LORD OF THE FLIES*

James R. Baker and Arthur P. Ziegler Jr., *Casebook Edition of William Golding's "Lord of the Flies."* New York: St. Martin's Press, 1965.

Jack Biles, *Talk: Conversations with William Golding.* Boston: Harcourt Brace Jovanovich, 1970.

John Carey, ed., *William Golding: The Man and His Books.* New York: Farrar, Straus & Giroux, 1987.

Bernard F. Dick, *William Golding.* Rev. ed. Boston: Twayne Publishers, 1987.

James Gindin, *William Golding.* Basingstoke and London: Macmillan, 1988.

Luke Grande, "The Appeal of Golding," *Commonweal*, January 25, 1963, pp. 457–59.

Suzanne Gulbin, "Parallels and Contrasts in *Lord of the Flies* and *Animal Farm*," *English Journal* 55, January 1966.

Samuel Hynes, *William Golding.* Columbia Essays on Modern Writers, no. 2. New York: Columbia University Press, 1964.

Frank Kermode and William Golding. "The Meaning of It All," *Books and Bookmen* 5, October 1959, pp. 9–10.

William Nelson, ed., *William Golding's* Lord of the Flies: *A Source Book.* New York: Odyssey Press, 1963.

Norman Page, ed., *William Golding: Novels, 1954–67.* Basingstoke and London: Macmillan, 1985.

Patrick Reilly, Lord of the Flies: *Fathers and Sons.* New York: Twayne Publishers, 1992.

John S. Whitley, *Golding: "Lord of the Flies."* Studies in English Literature, no. 42. London: Edward Arnold, 1970.

Raymond Wilson, *Lord of the Flies.* Macmillan Master Guides. Basingstoke and London: Macmillan, 1986.

ABOUT WORLD WAR II AND EUROPE DURING GOLDING'S LIFETIME

Bruce Bliven Jr., *The Story of D-Day: June 6, 1944.* New York: Random House, 1956.

Brent Engelmann, *In Hitler's Germany: Everyday Life in the Third Reich.* Trans. Krishna Winston. New York: Schocken Books, 1986.

Chris Fairclough, *We Live in Britain.* New York: Bookwright Press, 1984.

Barbara Fullers, *Cultures of the World: Britain.* New York: Marshall Cavendish, 1994.

Christopher Hibbert, *The English: A Social History 1066–1945.* New York: W.W. Norton, 1987.

John Irwin, *Modern Britain: An Introduction.* London: Archon Books, 1976.

John Keegan, *Six Armies in Normandy: From D-Day to the Liberation of Paris, June 6th–August 25th, 1944.* New York: Viking Press, 1982.

Larry Kimmett and Margaret Regis, *The Attack on Pearl Harbor: An Illustrated History.* Seattle, WA: Navigator Publishing, 1991.

David G. McCullough, ed., *The American Heritage Picture History of World War II.* New York: American Heritage Publishing Company, 1966.

Gerald Reitlinger, *The Final Solution: The Attempt to Exterminate the Jews of Europe 1939–1945.* New York: Thomas Yosetoff, 1953.

Gabriel Sempill, *Celtic Inheritance.* New York: Dorset Press, 1992.

Manfred Weidhorn, *Sir Winston Churchill.* Boston: Twayne Publishers, 1979.

WORKS BY WILLIAM GOLDING

Poems (1934)

Lord of the Flies (1954)

The Inheritors (1955)

Pincher Martin (1956); published in the United States as *The Two Lives of Christopher Martin* (1957)

The Brass Butterfly, a play (1958)

Free Fall (1959)

Book reviews for the *Spectator* (1960–1962)

Miss Pulkinhorn, a BBC radio script (April 20, 1960)

Break My Heart, a BBC radio script (March 19, 1961)

The Spire (1964)

The Hot Gates and Other Occasional Pieces, a book of essays (1966)

The Pyramid (1967)

The Scorpion God (1971)

Darkness Visible (1979)

Rites of Passage (1980)

A Moving Target, a book of essays (1982)

The Paper Men (1984)

An Egyptian Journal (1985)

Close Quarters (1987)

Fire Down Below (1989)

Index